Intropreneur

Strategies to Build your Business
as an Introverted Entrepreneur

Jen Jones

Green Heart Living Press

Intropreneur: Strategies to Build your Business as an Introverted Entrepreneur
Copyright © 2022 Jen Jones

ISBN Paperback: 978-1-954493-19-3

Cover Design by Barb Pritchard of Infinity Brand Design

Cover Photo Credit: Christine McShane of Christine McShane Creative

Dedication

Dedicated to my husband, my children, and to all those women who are introverted entrepreneurs.

My wish for my fellow intropreneurs is that you will find a new way to live that fills your soul, brings you joy and gives you energy and time back to your family.

Table of Contents

Foreword   7

Introduction   11

Part I: Aligning with Your Introverted Self   **15**

Chapter 1: The Authentic Introvert   17

Chapter 2: The Four Types of Introverts   23

Chapter 3: The Gifts of Introverts   34

Chapter 4: Evaluating Your Life Circles   43

Part II: Energy Awareness   **51**

Chapter 5: The Introvert's Energy Toolkit   53

Chapter 6: Being a Mom/Introvert/Entrepreneur   74

Part III: Growing Your Business   **83**

Chapter 7: Go Deep Not Wide   85

Chapter 8: Love Up Your Community   95

Chapter 9: Re-Imagining the Follow-Up   100

Chapter 10: Introverts are *Good* at Networking   112

Chapter 11: The Power of Online Groups   117

Part IV: Getting Comfortable with Shining Your Light   **125**

Chapter 12: Relationship Referral Strategy   127

Chapter 13: Collaborations   137

Chapter 14: Getting Started   141

Foreword

Nancy Anger

I put on a brave face and walked into the networking event trying to stay open-minded and optimistic. Maybe this would be the day I would figure out how to make new meaningful connections amidst a group of strangers, in a way that felt good to me!

To be honest, I was feeling out of my element and wondering if I would leave feeling overwhelmed, exhausted and disappointed once again.

As I stepped into the room, a woman stepped forward to greet me with a welcoming smile. She asked me a few questions and I felt like she was really listening to my answers which felt really good. I felt seen and heard.

Then I learned that she was a realtor and I was in the market for a new property! We had something in common! Maybe this wouldn't be so bad after all.

The woman who greeted me that day was Jen Jones. As I write this, I feel an unexpected surge of emotion and tears of gratitude for our meeting that day. A meeting that has blossomed into a beautiful relationship that includes both business and friendship!

What I didn't know that day is that Jen and I have

something else in common. We are both introverts and entrepreneurs. She gets it! The way we do business, create relationships and use our energy is different from our more extroverted counterparts.

When I started my business in early 2002 teaching yoga classes in the basement of a church, that too was out of my comfort zone. But I knew I had something important to share and my message was stronger than my fear, so I did it!

Over time, those classes grew into a full blown yoga and wellness center.

I remember sometimes asking myself, 'How did I, a stay at home, hermit mother get here?'

I didn't have the outgoing personality of my husband (who also had his own business). And while I was passionate about what I was doing, I didn't have the desire or energy to focus all my attention on my business. I wanted to have time to spend with my family and enjoy the other things that were important to me.

I also learned early on that everything in my life and business worked best when I gave myself regular alone time to rest and renew my energy!

And so that is how I built my business...and it worked perfectly for me.

Over the years, I taught hundreds of classes, spoke on

stage and in front of groups large and small, took multiple trainings and even traveled around the world for some of them. I was well-known in the community and had cultivated a wonderful circle of friends, clients and colleagues.

Then a few years ago, I sold my Yoga and Wellness Center to take my business online and things changed in ways I hadn't considered. While I still had many wonderful relationships, the community I had cultivated over the years was gone with the sale.

While I was excited about my new business as an Intuitive Coach and Energy Healer, I felt like I was starting over again in many ways! The thought of finding and/or creating a new community started to feel overwhelming!

When I walked into the networking event that day and met Jen, little did I know the wonderful impact that one new relationship would have on my life!

Jen has not only served as a reminder of the things I had learned while building my wellness center that I had somehow lost sight of or stopped trusting on some level, she also gave me a whole set of new tools and ideas that have helped me appreciate and rethink how I make connections and build my business, in a way that feels like me!

She is a wife, mother, entrepreneur and a master at building authentic connections and creating wonderful collaborative communities. And she does it all, introvert style!

Jen Jones is a role model and wayshower helping introverted entrepreneurs find success in their businesses in ways that honor their energy, natural abilities and their values!

I am excited about Jen Jones' book *Intropreneur*, which brings it all together so beautifully! The guidance she provides reminds me of how I was able to build my first business and so much more. What I had to figure out by trial-and-error, she has laid out for introverts to know ahead of time, so they can build their business — without feeling depleted or overwhelmed.

I am excited to see how this book will help many other introverts build their businesses.

While networking events are still not my preferred way of making new connections, Jen has shared so many ideas and perspectives to use that enhance my natural way of doing business and building meaningful relationships. I now enjoy my business with more of the ease and flow I created in my first business with plenty of time for naps or just BEing :-)!

Grab a cup of tea and enjoy.

Nancy Anger
Spiritual Teacher, Intuitive Guide and Master Energy Healer

Introduction

After having my third baby, ten years after my last, it took me a few months to recover. I was a little older and a lot more tired. I also needed to find some friends that had babies the same age. So I joined the local Moms Club, which was one of the best things I did. I connected with some amazing moms, who were also entrepreneurs. I am all about supporting other women, so I created the Mompreneur Facebook group in October 2015. It was a place to connect on a personal level, share our expertise, and network with each other.

We took this to the next level and started meeting in person. There weren't any local opportunities to network with other women, especially when we all had little ones in tow, so we found a way to make it happen. We would meet at my house and everyone pitched in $5/kid for 90 minutes for childcare. A mom who didn't have a business was able to bring her kids and make some money, while watching our kids. We were a group of moms helping moms.

It was during these meetings I realized I reignited my love to teach about doing business by referrals and repeat business, time management, and connecting. My heart was helping women entrepreneurs better their business and personal lives in a way that felt good to them. I also knew I would eventually write a book. What I wasn't prepared for were the lessons and realizations along this writing journey. It's like taking a magnifying glass on your process, your business, your life, and whatever lessons are meant for you, they will appear.

This book has been in my heart for a few years now. The opportunity came up and I was "in" — or so I thought. My book writing process brought up lessons that needed to be learned and shared, which you will find throughout this book.

Being a woman and an introverted entrepreneur has its challenges on many levels. I found myself getting stuck in proving myself as a Broker/Owner of a real estate company. If I wasn't selling as much as so and so, I would fear everyone was going to think I was not successful. It took me a good year to figure out what my goal was for the business. At the time, it was being home for my kids when they got off the bus in the afternoon, being home for dinner most nights, and sending my littlest to day care only 2-3 times a week. There were money goals, too, that allowed me to have flexibility in my life and business so I could move my business forward while being there for my family. Defining my own success took a while to figure out. Even with this book, sharing my failures that turned into lessons and opportunity for growth has been difficult.

This book came to be through trial and error. After more than 18 years in the real estate industry and over two years as a coach/consultant, I found there is a way that makes sense for introverted women who are entrepreneurs to fulfill their business and lives.

I invite you to learn from my experiences and your own. This will speed up the process of getting you from where you are right now to where you want to be. Using the process and tools in this book, you will be brought through the pillars of a fulfilled and joyful Intropreneur. The pillars are: Aligning with Your Introverted Self, Energy Awareness, Growing Your Business through Joyful Relationships, and Getting Comfortable with Shining Your Light.

As you move through the book, there will be areas you know well and then there are areas you will want to work on. I encourage you to scan through the Table of Contents and jump in.

In Part I, we'll take a look at aligning our hearts with our minds and actions. As there is not a one size fits all when it comes to us introverts, I can't wait for you to identify with one of the four types of introverts. We will also explore the gifts of an introvert. You may be surprised at the beautiful gifts you have as an introvert that you may have previously viewed as weaknesses.

In Part II, we'll test your energy awareness by evaluating and identifying what works best for you when it comes to your energy management. We will also find your "optimal" time to be productive and how it can work for you.

Part III is about growing your business through joyful relationships. This is where you can really shine as an introvert by using those introvert gifts, especially the gift of having the ability to create and nurture deep relationships by going deep not wide, tap into your innate ability to follow up, network like an introvert and use online groups for these relationships.

Part IV is where we tie it all together with referrals, repeat business, and collaborations. This is also where we go over the Relationship Referral Strategy that aligns your heart with your mind and actions!

Using this book as your framework to create or grow your business in a way that is aligned with your introverted self and is life-fulfilling, which also means your business is fulfilling.

Enjoy bringing all of this together for a life and business you want!

XOXO
Jen

-1-

Aligning With
Your Introverted Self

Chapter 1

The Authentic Introvert

I have heard people say "fake it til you make it." And, frankly, that used to be one of my favorite things to say (and do). There were times I'd have to psych myself up to go and meet new people, whether I was meeting up with an entire group or just one other person. By the time I would arrive, I had revved myself up and I was ready to conquer the room. Almost every time I would do this, it was inevitable that there were hours spent "rejuvenating" my energy. And I was showing up as a different version of myself which felt very fake.

I've come to realize this was me putting on my "extrovert hat." If you're an introvert, you know what I am talking about! The "extrovert hat" transforms you from the boring, quiet, shy introvert into the outgoing, energetic extrovert. That's what it is all about. Fake it til you make it! Well, I am here to tell you this burnt me out and left me with no energy for hours if not days later.

Several years ago, I decided that if I wanted to have a successful business and relationships it had to be the real me, no more masks. I needed to tap into my authentic self—the one who at times is the quietest in the room. I would not consider myself shy, as would many introverts I know. Shyness is typically associated with introverts, but not all introverts are shy! I may be the one who thinks for a few minutes/hours to respond to someone's request or question. Or I might have only met one person during an event. Realizing these are gifts made connecting with people more authentic for me. Being my introverted self attracted so many of the right people, who are still in my life today!

I knew in order to move my business forward, I needed to align with my introverted self. You might be wondering, *How do I do that?* Or, you might be thinking, *I'm already aligned with myself.* In either case, I encourage you to read on because we are ever changing beings. Just when I think I have complete alignment, something shifts that I need to adjust to and settle into. You may find the same to be true for you as well.

As I wrote this book, there were so many alignment shifts that I can't even begin to share them all. What I will share right now is how to align with your introverted self. Maybe for some this is just a review. I am happy you've done that inner work to get to where you are right now. Keep it up!

If you are looking to be more aligned and feel like you haven't gotten there yet, please pay close attention. Why is it so important to be true to yourself and the outside world? Being your introverted self allows you to be vulnerable and have deep, meaningful relationships. I'm not just talking about your business but also other areas of your life, including with your significant other, family, friends, etc. Being authentic leads to deep, meaningful relationships in our lives which brings us greater joy and fulfillment. Doesn't that sound delightful?

The following questions will help you uncover your introverted self. Answer yourself honestly, no one is seeing your answers.

How to Uncover Your Authentic Self

"In order for connection to happen, we have to allow ourselves to be seen, really seen." - Brené Brown

Set aside some alone time where it is quiet, you are ready to listen to yourself, and open to what may come to you.

Ask yourself the following questions:

- What brings me joy in my life and business? List in priority your top 5-10.

- Do your actions and thoughts align with your beliefs and values?

- How do things you do and think make you feel in your core/gut/intuition?

- What feelings come up when you think about your introverted self?

After answering these questions, there may have been some things that came up for you that you need to process. I'd recommend setting it aside, taking time to process, and coming back to it tomorrow. You may want to consider meditating or journaling about these questions and answers.

We can move onto the feeling that comes over you when you are being authentic. Maybe you felt it when you were answering some of the questions.

What Does it Feel Like to Be Authentic?

When you are being authentic, you can feel content, calm, and at peace. You feel like you are not people-pleasing, or at least that is for me. It's when you LOVE who you are in all situations. You are confident in yourself. You are in a place where you can be yourself without fear of people judging you or thinking you are less than. This doesn't mean you won't ever feel these things again. The more we practice being vulnerable, feeling, and being aware of those times when we are ourselves and acknowledge how good it really feels in the moment, that's when you know you are YOU, ever-evolving and shifting.

Aligning with who you are, think about the times when you have been alone and imagine what you think about and contemplate. Think about how others describe you. Being authentic is a state of being where you are comfortable in your own skin and it does not deplete your energy.

For me, life looks a lot different as I have prioritized myself, protected my energy, and shared with other introverts how I did it. I feel amazing (most days).

When we are being our authentic introverted self, we are comfortable in our own skin. How we feel about ourselves may be a bit vulnerable. This can be hard, especially if you are a recovering perfectionist! Making mistakes, sharing our lives and businesses is vulnerable, scary, and can also open the door to judgment by others. In the end, sharing our vulnerabilities shows we have truly accepted and love ourselves.

There may be times when we doubt we are being authentic. It could just be fear getting in your head or maybe you've veered off and back to old habits. Old habits surely die hard. As an introvert, I feel as though it can be hard to show people who I am in fear they won't like me, think I am weird, too quiet, too shy, not interested, or not interesting.

The more authentic in all areas of your life, the more aligned and natural being yourself becomes.

Contemplating if you are an introvert or not? I have met many people who either haven't heard about introverts or they aren't really sure if they are one. This reiterates the need for this book and getting it into the hands of every introvert (or those who aren't sure, so they can figure it out). Once you know, it is empowering to use this new knowledge to shift and upgrade yourself, your life, and your business.

How You Know You Are an Introvert

The ultimate determining question is: Do you get your energy from retreating and being alone? Then you are an introvert!

Still not sure? Let's ask a few more questions.

- When asked for your opinion or thoughts on something do you usually need a few minutes to ponder your answer?

- Do you despise small talk?

- Does your energy get lowered when meeting new people?

- Are you a good listener?

- Do you have a small group of friends that you can "be yourself with?"

If you are nodding your head *Yes!* as you read these, I am 99.9% sure you are an introvert.

Chapter 2

The Four Types of Introverts

I first learned about the different types of introverts when I read Jenn Granneman's book *The Secret Lives of Introverts.*[1] In this book, Jenn introduces the STAR survey, developed by Jonathan Cheek, a Professor and Psychologist at Wellesley College, and graduate students Jennifer Grimes and Courtney Brown.[2]

STAR stands for Social, Thinking, Anxious, and Restrained. These are the four types of introverts that Creek and his students discovered after surveying about 500 adults. As in most surveys and personality quizzes, there's no guarantee it will hit the nail on the head. But I have found the STAR survey really gives an eye-opening view of what type you may be. The results may be shocking, interesting, or just a confirmation of what you already know.

The Four Types of Introverts

Social Introversion - Some people may get the wrong

---

[1] Granneman, Jenn. *The Secret Lives of Introverts.*
[2] Cheek, Jonathan M., Courtney Al. Brown, and Jennifer O. Grimes. *Personality Scales for Four Domains of Introversion: Social, Thinking, Anxious, and Restrained Introversion. Wellesley, MA: Department of Psychology, Wellesley College, 2014. htps://www.academia.edu/7353616*

idea when they hear the term social introvert. Social introversion is when you like to be around small groups but there's a twist. In many cases as a social introvert, you like to know most of the people in the group, you don't necessarily want to spend all day with them, and you definitely need alone time.

This is the form of introversion that I most identify with myself. In my personal experience, there have been times when a small group has given me a burst of energy afterwards but I always seem to need downtime/alone time at some point.

With social introversion, a distinction is made that the time alone isn't because of shyness or anxiety but about being in crowds or around other people. It's just that we need some rejuvenation time.

As Cheek explains, "They prefer to stay home with a book or a computer, or to stick to small gatherings with close friends, as opposed to attending large parties with many strangers."

Thinking Introversion - Thinking introverts are introspective, thoughtful, and self-reflective. Thinking introverts use imagination and creativity.

"You're capable of getting lost in an internal fantasy world," explains Cheek. "But it's not in a neurotic way, it's in an imaginative and creative way."

Anxious Introversion - Anxious introverts have an aversion to gatherings and small groups. Anxious introverts seek out alone time because they feel awkward and self-conscious about their social skills and ability to be around other people. Their mind takes over and plays the reel over and over and over again, ruminating about what disaster did, could, or may happen in social situations. They may have trouble shutting their minds off. They may be up during the night thinking about the things that went wrong today, last week, or maybe even last year. They have trouble shutting off negative thoughts.

Restrained Introversion - This could be a "reserved" introvert. They have lower energy and are slow to get moving. They aren't the type to hop out of bed and get on with their day. They think before they speak or act.

The STAR Survey[3]

Fill in the blank next to each item with one of the following choices:

1 = very uncharacteristic or untrue, strongly disagree
2 = uncharacteristic
3 = neutral
4 = characteristic
5 = very characteristic or true, strongly agree

[3] The STAR Survey was developed by Jonathan Cheek, Courtney Brown and Jennifer Grimes and was abbreviated by Jenn Granneman.

Social Introversion

_____ 1. I like to share special occasions with just one person or a few close friends, rather than have big celebrations.

_____ 2. I try to structure my day so that I always have some time to myself.

_____ 3. My ideal vacation involves lots of time to relax by myself.

_____ 4. After spending a few hours surrounded by a lot of people, I am usually eager to get away by myself.

_____ 5. I usually prefer to do things alone.

_____ 6. Other people tend to misunderstand me – forming a mistaken impression of what kind of person I am because I don't say much about myself.

_____ 7. I feel drained after social situations, even when I enjoy myself.

Thinking Introversion

_____ 1. I enjoy analyzing my own thoughts and ideas about myself.

_____ 2. I have a rich, complex inner life.

_____ 3. I frequently think about what kind of person I am.

_____ 4. When I am reading an interesting story or novel, or when I am watching a good movie, I imagine how I would feel if the events in the story were happening to me.

_____ 5. I generally pay attention to my inner feelings.

_____ 6. I sometimes step back (in my mind) in order to examine myself from a distance.

_____ 7. I daydream and fantasize with some regularity about things that might happen to me.

Anxious Introversion

_____ 1. When I enter a room, I often become self-conscious and feel that the eyes of others are upon me.

_____ 2. My thoughts are often focused on episodes of my life that I wish I'd stop thinking about.

_____ 3. My nervous system sometimes feels so frazzled that I just have to go off by myself.

_____ 4. I don't feel very confident about my social skills.

_____ 5. Defeat or disappointment usually shame or anger me, but I try not to show it.

_____ 6. It takes me some time to overcome my shyness in new situations.

_____ 7. Even when I am in a group of friends, I often feel very alone and uneasy.

Restrained Introversion

_____ 1. I have a hard time getting moving when I wake up in the morning.

_____ 2. For relaxation, I like to slow down and take things easy.

_____ 3. I am often slow to speak, thinking carefully about what I say before I say it.

_____ 4. It's very hard for me to step out of my comfort zone. I rarely seek new experiences and sensations.

_____ 5. Being busy stresses me out.

_____ 6. I need plenty of time to think before I act.

_____ 7. I usually stop and think things over before making a decision.

How Did You Do?

To find out your score, add together all of your answers for each set of seven items to come up with your total score for each type. Here's a guide of how you scored compared to others in the general population:

Social Introversion
If you scored below 17, you are low in social introversion. If you scored around 21, you are average in social introversion. If you scored above 25, you are high in social introversion.

Thinking Introversion
Low: Below 18
Average: Around 21
High: Above 24

Anxious Introversion
Low: Below 15
Average: Around 19
High: Above 23

Restrained Introversion
Low: Below 15
Average: Around 20
High: Above 25

What to Do with Your Results

When I completed the quiz, the highest score was "Social Introvert" and second highest was "Thinking Introvert." This affirmed what I already knew.

Knowing the type of introvert that you most align your energy with will allow you to evaluate your current schedule, work, communication styles, and relationships to align with your introversion type. You can work with your introvert type, rather than fighting against it.

After reviewing my first and second introversion types, it made me realize why I have identified as an ambivert in the past. Some may be wondering what the heck an ambivert is! The Merriam-Webster dictionary defines an ambivert as "a person having characteristics of both extrovert and introvert."

In my heart, it feels more true to say that I am a social and thinking introvert. In the past, saying I am an introvert felt weak and not exciting. Using my 'extrovert hat' was a way to get out there and grow my business like everyone else. It left me exhausted and needing to retreat to gain back my energy. In most cases, I didn't make the time to rejuvenate, mostly because I packed my schedule like sardines and was raising young kids so there was very little opportunity to leave white space, which I will be talking about later in the book. There really was no time to take care of me. I needed to just keep going. I look back at that time in my life and wonder, *how did I survive the constant hustle and grinding in business and life?*

As I reflect on the past decade, I've moved very slowly

to shift the hustle and grind mentality. The desire to practice more flow and ease. It is a challenge to balance the doing and the being! It is a practice that I consciously have everyday to be present in the moment.

The hustle and grind mentality brings with it the myth of multitasking, along with other things we won't get into here. But I'm a believer that we can only truly focus on one thing at a time and there are ways to create a life and business that works for you, not against you. I realized this on such a deep level when a close friend said to me, "Have you tried working out without having the TV on?" This comment shocked me at the time. Being efficient is one of my superpowers, so I thought!

I tried working out and not doing anything else. My mind was blown when I realized I was distracted by the TV. I could actually feel the muscles that I was using, my heart rate was up a bit more and I was burning more calories. If it wasn't for this lesson, I would not have looked at other areas of my life where I was thinking I was being efficient, when in fact, I was multitasking with less efficiency.

Another time, I had gotten a new book and I couldn't wait to crack it open and start reading it. My little guy had his first ninja warrior class, so I thought I'd just read while he was doing his thing. We got there and I didn't read at all. What I realized is this was another moment when I was "being efficient" when in actuality reading would have led me to miss all the moments during that class for my little guy. On a deep cellular level, I also realized I do this in my life a lot and you know what, I've been missing out on my life!

I'd be lying if I said this didn't hit me hard, like I cried, hard. It was so sad at the moment of this awakening. Thinking I've been "practicing" being present and it took someone saying, "Have you tried working out without having the TV on?" to make me aware of where I might be doing this and missing out on my life!

I used to feel like I was on a hamster wheel all the time. It still feels like this sometimes, but now I am more aware and more prepared to make necessary shifts when I feel this way. It's easier to get back on track in life and business. This makes me feel more joyful and grounded. Hence the story I told you about efficiency.

When we start to look at all aspects of our lives, we begin to evaluate what is working and what is not. It gives us the opportunity to shift priorities, if needed. In addition, it allows for reflection when we are able to take a step back. It gives us space to figure out what we want life to feel and look like. We started our own business for a reason!

Why do you own your business? What were the reasons you became an entrepreneur? For me, it was the flexibility that I could have in order to make life work with kids. Being home when the kiddos got off the bus was really important to me.

In the day-to-day of life and business, the reason you started your business becomes less in the forefront because we get caught up in the tasks, goals, and results. These are important too! As you focus on these things, keep your reason front and center, your why, your vision for your life, your lifestyle dream. Most importantly, keep how you want to feel in your lifestyle dream. If you get caught up in the doing and forget the being, your reality will look different than your vision.

This is definitely not how I ran my business and my life over a decade ago. I let my business rule me and ultimately created a life I no longer wanted. I was working all the time, I was meeting with people all the time, my battery was always in the red. I barely slept. I ran on adrenaline for years. One day it all came tumbling down. I needed to change how I was running my business and my life. I was so in the grind and hustle, not thinking about the lifestyle that I really wanted. The focus was more on the day-to-day achievements than the big lifestyle dream. I realized my business/career was not what made me worthy. My achievements weren't the only things that should have mattered. I had limiting beliefs that weren't true, like I'm not a good mom. I defined myself with the accomplishments of my work and it was the only place that I felt worthy.

What I finally realized a few years ago was that if I used my introvert gifts then I would feel more into the being than the doing. This past year has shown me having more time to Be will show you the way to the life and business in your vision.

Chapter 3

The Gifts of Introverts

Your introvert gifts guide you to align with your introvert self. There are so many introvert gifts, I've decided to choose a few to dive deeper. This chapter is meant for you to read and reflect on each gift. There is a range of having all of these gifts to having just a couple. After each section, make a note of any gifts that you identify as your own.

Leader/Team Player

Have you or someone close to you recognized the Leader/Team Player Introvert Gift in you?

I was going to separate these two into their own sections but realized that in many ways we can be both, so I kept them together like peanut butter and jelly!

When I think about leaders and leadership, I certainly don't automatically think about a person who is an introvert. Many leaders we first think about are the ones who are outgoing, have a "following," maybe even a little flashy, charismatic. There are some negative words to describe leaders in our society but I'd rather focus on describing why it is important to discuss the introvert gift of leader/team players. I have witnessed time and time again that introvert leaders listen to their people and allow everyone to be heard. This is also the case of a team player, as usually they are either the lead of the team or they are the right-hand person to the leader. Allowing everyone to be heard is such a gift and a strength, especially when building a community (online or in-person), leading or participating in a collaboration and/or movement.

If this is one of your introvert gifts, then I would highly recommend one or more of the following: Collaboration, partnership, starting a podcast or being a guest on a podcast, producing an online show, bring people together in person or on zoom with a workshop, training, mastermind, panel, host your own networking event, these are just a few ideas to think about.

These gifts will sometimes stand alone, others will stack.

Reflection

Let's reflect! Introverts have a way of taking information and really thinking deep about it. Introverts not only think deeply, but they will brainstorm, come up with innovative ideas, and create action plans. A key to allowing this gift to flourish is to give yourself time to think and reflect. Although many introverts are challenged with speaking on their feet, when you have the time to reflect it allows you to give an answer that is not induced by stress. If you are in a conversation with someone but need a bit more time to think/pause, a couple good tools you can use are: 1) Saying, "Tell me more." 2) Express how grateful you are that they confided in you and let them know you will give it some deep thought and get back to them, then set up a 1:1 or date that you will follow-up.

Not being able to give immediate feedback or come up with an idea on the spot does not mean you are unsuccessful or not able to contribute. This is because you have the gift of deep thinking and reflection. Don't hesitate to say that you would like to reflect on what they said and provide feedback via email (or other form of communication). You can say, "nothing is coming to me at the moment, but it's usually at 2 am when I'll get a ping."

Speaking of pings and reflections, deep-thinking introverts can find themselves in their own thoughts during the day or even in the middle of the night. I know I am not the only one out there that wakes up at 2 am having the most amazing idea, imagining/dreaming of conversations with people expressing our thoughts openly, freely and with ease.

Calming Energy

This leads us into the next introvert gift, Calming Energy. Calming Energy puts people at ease and attracts them to you because you make them feel safe to share with you and be in your energy. You are seen as a trustworthy person. It allows people to open up to you, nurture deeper, meaningful relationships. This Calming Energy can also be seen in difficult situations. You are someone that easily diffuses these situations. You may not realize this gift in yourself or maybe you aren't an introvert that has calming energy. I certainly didn't think this was me until several people had mentioned how calm I am when faced with certain situations. Do you see this gift in yourself? If not, look deeper. Ask a close friend or family member they see things in us that we are too blind to realize, at times.

This kind of energy allows you to be the calm in the storm. In many cases, a situation like this elevates you and you become a great leader. See how these gifts intertwine with each other? You may not see all of these gifts in yourself, but what I do hope is you can sit and contemplate what introvert gifts you do have and ask yourself, "am I using them for my highest good?"

Focused Alone Time

Do you have the ability to focus alone for long periods of time? Do you get so absorbed in a project that you forget to eat, drink, or get a good night's sleep? This gift of focus gives us creative juices, ideas, the ability to get more done in less time, the ability to solve problems, and ultimately can allow us to become experts. This time alone focusing on one thing brings forth greater awareness and aligned outcomes. Looking back, when you spent an extended amount of alone time, what did you accomplish?

You may also use this focused time for yourself. This time for yourself can help you recharge, reflect on a situation, or give you the space you need to make a decision. Carving out this time for yourself is important for your overall well-being, mentally, physically, emotionally and your energy. We'll dive deep into your energy rejuvenation and awareness in Chapter 5.

You can also use your focused alone time to learn something new. Introverts are well-versed in learning new things on their own, preferably an online course, YouTube, etc. This time can be internally motivating, which leads to things getting done, creative flow moving at quantum speed, and with intense focus.

Highly Sensitive & Hyper Observant

Are you highly sensitive? Do you take on other people's emotions? Are you hyper observant? Do you like to people-watch?

Let's take a look at these gifts in a bit more detail. Do you notice when people are angry, frustrated, sad or irritated? Maybe you observe shifts in the person you are talking to, because you are paying attention and are picking up on the person's emotions.

This gift also makes people feel comfortable with you, like calming energy, you can empathize with someone. You are able to really put yourself in their shoes. You may take this introvert gift for granted, but not everyone can do this. This can also take a toll on your own emotions and energy, so be aware that you aren't taking on other people's energy, as this can drain you. Know when you need to step away and recharge, or even step away so you can better protect yourself, your emotions and energy.

During a workshop, I was talking about the gift of being hyper-observant and gave the example of people watching. Most of the people laughed and shared that they are also people watchers. Yes, I mean from the sidelines but also actively being observant. As you talk to people you tend to read their body language. When you are in a room full of people, you can pick out the people that you want to approach and get to know better. There's not usually that many in the room an introvert wants to approach but these people have a specific vibe you pick up on that matches your energy. This leads us into the next gift so beautifully.

Extremely Supportive

Being extremely supportive is one of my most favorite gifts, simply because I have seen it time and time again among clients, groups I belong to, and out in the world. Introverts have an innate way of being extremely supportive and show up for their people. It doesn't matter if they are introverts or not, the deep relationships that introverts nurture bring forth a community willing to help each other in any way possible. Witnessing this gift warms my heart and I am grateful to be part of many communities and groups that support others and I get to support in return.

I connect this gift to the innate ability introverts have to create deep, lasting relationships. Once you get to know someone, you have connected on an emotional level. So whether it is business or personal, you are there to support them however you are able. I've seen support come in many ways, a gift package for someone who was going through a hard time with her family, tremendous support after having a baby, a Summit that was promoted to so many people via social media and email. The list goes on!

Deep, Lasting Relationship-Nurturer

You create deep, lasting relationships. This gift gives you the opportunity to not put people into boxes, the friend box and the biz relationship box. It all meshes together, just like you don't separate your personal life with your business. This feels natural to include all the people you want to surround yourself with in one circle. You care for the people in your circle by nurturing your relationships, asking questions about their families, personal life, and their business if they have one. You make notes to not forget some of the important details of their lives.

It may not come easily to you but making new friends is a great way to connect your circle to new people. You never know who will connect with each other, and that person could have the right connections needed.

Introverts listen when others are talking and have deep conversations. No small talk for us! When two introverts get together and they know each other well, the excitement, the talking, the connection is powerful! On the outside, you probably look like an extrovert, but in the deep conversation, you both are listening (yet taking turns talking). It almost feels like magic because you are comfortable with this person that you can talk about all the things and hold space for them to do the same and offer feedback.

As introverts, we have to realize that the things we have to offer to this world are AMAZING. It's no surprise that we often see these gifts as weaknesses. We usually see the extroverts working the room, being leaders with charisma, etc. Extroverts are viewed positively while introverts are seen as weak, shy, quiet, but these are beliefs that need to shift. That is not to say that extroverts don't have their own set of gifts. They do, but introverts are not weak. After going through some of the ones I highlighted, I wanted to share more of these gifts, so you can see how special and gifted you are as an introvert.

Here are some of the other introvert gifts that I have identified in myself, clients, friends, and family:

- We are trustworthy.

- We are great listeners, we'd rather hear about others than talk about ourselves.

- We think deeply.

- We rarely get bored.

- We have interesting lives.

- We like working alone or in a team.

- We are problem-solvers.

- We come up with unique ideas.

- We are persistent.

- We are experts in our fields because we do our research.

- We are consistent.

Identifying your introvert gifts expands your thinking about your strengths. Some of these gifts you may have thought were weaknesses. By shining the light on them, it brings in a new perspective. This new perspective can bring you confidence, joy, and a greater passion for your life and business.

After attending one of my workshops, Nicole (owner of Just a Nibble Bakery) shared, "I'm hoping to focus more on my traits as a positive instead of a negative." This is a practice and the identification of these traits as gifts is a first step.

Guiding people through the process of identifying their introvert gifts is a real passion for me. It brings me so much joy.

In the next chapter, we will look at evaluating your life circles and how you define success.

Chapter 4

Evaluating Your Life Circles

This is a great opportunity to slow down, take in what you have read so far, and evaluate where you are in all areas of your life.

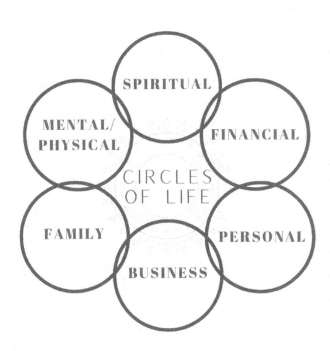

Are you completely fulfilled in your life and business? Are you living the lifestyle you want? The lifestyle that you imagine and feel excited about when you sit and dream. We will evaluate six life circles that consist of: Personal, Business, Financial, Physical/Mental, Spiritual, and Family.

In my opinion, working on one area at a time is important. For example, if I am starting a new workout/eat-healthy plan to lose 40 pounds, it probably isn't a good idea to also grow your business by 25%. Now, this isn't a free pass to not have goals in all areas but to make your goals smaller in the other areas. Your energy awareness matters! If you start to focus on too many areas, your efficiency goes down.

Listen to your intuition when you are evaluating and setting your goals. I advise you to feel into each of them and ask yourself questions: How does this make me feel? Is it joyful? Focus on the goals that bring you the most joy, happiness, and fulfillment.

Tracking your progress, reviewing your goals, adjusting them as you move through each month/quarter is important. You make the decision when to evaluate your goals by knowing the thresholds and milestones. There are times I have set goals and realized a couple months later that they weren't the goals that felt aligned for me, but didn't know it at the time. Once we get into the daily actions, this can help us realize the goals need to be adjusted. This is why periodic re-evaluation of goals is important.

Evaluating Your Life Circles

1. Rate each area here by using a rating scale 1-10 (1 being not fulfilling at all to a 10 being most fulfilling). This will give a quick snapshot of the areas that you are thriving in and the ones that need work.

   List your rating:

   - Personal -
   - Business -
   - Financial -
   - Physical/Mental -
   - Spiritual -
   - Family -

2. Identify the top 3 areas most in need of your attention. In the spirit of focusing on one thing at a time, pick one thing in each area that would raise your score at least 1-2 points.

   My top 3 areas are:

   -
   -
   -

3. Choose one that you want to focus on over the next 30 days.

   The one thing I would like to focus on over the next 30 days is:

4. Identify 1-3 action steps you can take to move forward in that circle.

   My Action Steps:

   -
   -
   -

5. After 30 days, evaluate and rate how you did, how do you feel? What do the next 30 days look like, maybe it is the same circle or you move onto the next.

   Reflection after first 30 days:

   Actions Steps for the next 30 days:
   -
   -
   -

Defining Success

How you define success can be an eye-opening experience that brings you closer to living authentically. As you go through the life circles, think about how you define success in each one.

This isn't what your industry says is success and it isn't what your coach or anyone else defines success, it is how you define it. *You* are the one who gets to choose what success is for you. That is a bold and confident statement. Say it out loud, **"I get to choose what success is for me."**

In the past, I was influenced by how others defined success. It has felt so freeing to define my own success. What I needed to do was let go of the outside judgment (or perceived judgment) of my success.

You will hear all the cultural sayings, "work hard, play hard," "hustle," "sacrifice to succeed." All of these have a negative connotation for me. Maybe they don't for you. That's okay! These words make me think of working for hours and hours, sacrificing family, friends, sleep, and time for yourself. Work until you can't work anymore! You'll sleep when you are dead! This is a recipe for disaster and burnout, especially for those of us who are perfectionists and overachievers. I invite you to be aware of these cultural norms and rethink your definition of success. Think about what you want in your life, more importantly, listen to your body and feel how great it will be to live in the feeling of your own success that you defined.

Intropreneur in Action

Kate's Story

Bringing people together is such an important part of networking, connecting, and collaborating. There are so many ways to build community. People come to me to learn how they can get out there enough to connect with clients so they can serve them. One of my clients Kate talks a little bit about getting out of her comfort zone.

"When I first started working with Jen, I had fallen into a pattern where I'd network and market like crazy, and then totally burnout and go into introvert-hiding. Jen helped me see what I was doing — trying to build my business using methods that worked for other people but didn't feel good to me.

Jen taught me how to build more sustainable habits, which gives me the energy to make strong connections with my clients and write insightful copy that sounds and feels like them. My business is now almost 100% referral, and demand for my services is so high that I've raised my prices and am STILL booking out weeks in advance."

-2-

Energy Awareness

Chapter 5

The Introvert's Energy Toolkit

Introverts get their energy by going inward and being alone. Recharging your energy is important for your self-care. Being aware of what depletes your energy is just as important. Some common things that deplete energy for introverts are your own thoughts, other people's energy, or being around people. Having tools will help you continue to be aware of your energy, how things in your life affect your energy, and what to do to rejuvenate your energy. These tools will help you grow and make shifts in your life where you need it the most.

Everyone has a way that works best to rejuvenate their energy. Do you know what works best for you? Over this past year, I have paid close attention to my energy. I have developed my awareness of what (and who) depletes my energy, what it will take to bring my energy level back to "sustainable" or "thriving" and how I can do this intentionally, on purpose.

There is a baseline energy you need for your day-to-day tasks, which I call "sustainable" energy. It's when you feel stable in your energy, not depleted after doing a few tasks, and can be brought back to sustainable energy fairly quickly with short Mini-Charges. These Mini-Charge activities are 1-15 minutes of an activity you have identified as a way to recharge quickly to bring you back to the "sustainable" status/level.

For example, I have a client that knows she gets recharged when she takes a walk in nature or is able to go outside and walk on her grass and breathe for a few minutes. It centers her in a way that allows for her energy to be quickly brought back up to the sustainable level. We will get into more details on this as we move through the chapter. What things or activities recharge your energy quickly?

"Thriving" is a state of being when you have filled all the leaks in your energy, been proactive with your time and energy, and you have habits that continue to raise your energy to "Thriving." To get to this state, you have prioritized and continue to make time for yourself in a way that brings forth full rejuvenation.

The Full-Charge Energy Design is for activities that take more than 15 minutes and you leave this activity with a feeling of euphoria (and it lasts). This is the goal, to be fully charged and rejuvenated so you can "Thrive" in life. The feeling you have when you are in this place exceeds your expectations. The most important part of this is knowing what works the best for you to get to the place of "Thriving."

Conserving energy by creating habits is one approach to your energy. I have personally found that I need buffers in my day. If I don't have a 30-minute break in between activities, I get exhausted and a Mini-Recharge won't cut it at the end of the day. Let me be clear, I am not perfect at this by any means and every time I do book things back to back, it's like that emoji with palm-to-face! One thing that I know will help is buffers in my schedule. These buffers are used to do a Mini-Charge activity, even if it is just breathing.

Another habit I have implemented is not to schedule more than three appointments in a day. I also do not schedule anything after an evening networking event, so I can honor my energy and go to bed. If it is in the middle of the day, I add a longer buffer of at least one hour before the next appointment.

We are all busy and there are times when this is not possible. When this happens, I invite you to bring in the awareness of how you are feeling, rate your energy (which we talk about more in the four steps below), and be sure to add what I call a "Full-Charge" to the end of your day. It will make all the difference in how you then move into the evening and the next day.

The Four Step Energy Toolkit

STEP 1: Pinpoint Energy Leaks

The first thing you must get clarity around is knowing what is depleting your energy. Think about those energy leaks throughout the day. Anything that requires too much interaction and stimulation is an energy leak for me and requires me to recharge after. What depletes your energy?

This is a great exercise to do for a week and figure out where your leaks are and rate your energy level along the way. This can help you become more aware of your energy level and what recharges it. Gather this information on activities throughout your day. As we move to the next steps, you will see how to keep your energy level productive and not depleted. I'd also challenge you to explore what thoughts you have that might be depleting your energy, too.

You will need to prepare to keep track of your activities (and thoughts, if you choose to do both). You will need some way of tracking. Some ideas: a journal, notebook, your notepad on your phone, your planner, or a spreadsheet. You can experiment to find what works best for you to track your activities and energy ratings, as shown.

Pinpoint Energy Leaks

Let's go through some activities you are already aware of that deplete your energy and rate them. Think about a day or two where you were completely exhausted. What activities were you engaging in? What thoughts were you having at the time? Did you jam-pack your schedule? Look at the variables that had an effect on your energy level. Take notes on all of this.

Rate your current energy level (1-5):

1= Exhausted and need to retreat to bed
3= You need a little boost of energy
5= Excited and energized to move to the next thing

Need some examples to jog your memory? Here are some examples that my clients and I have experienced.

Examples of depleting activities:

- Too many people needing your attention at once.

- Interacting with new people either 1:1 or in groups.

- Not having enough alone time.

- Packing your day with high-energy activities.

- Too much on your schedule.

- Carrying too much in your brain at once.

- Lots of expectations.

- Anything that requires interaction with a lot of people or too many stimulations at one time.

- Thoughts that are self-sabotaging.

Take a few minutes to add to this list. What activities deplete your energy?

As school for the kids finished up for the year, I was sitting in reflection and realized how much energy was being used on a daily basis just to be at home with my daughter who was learning remotely. She was a self-sufficient 10th grader thriving with remotely learning. So why did I feel so exhausted? It dawned on me the week school was ending how much energy was being sucked from me by having her home. I don't know any other way to explain it. I realized in hindsight that I would have felt much less depleted if I had packed up my laptop and backpack and went to the coffee house, where I used to spend time working outside of the house. BUT I DID NOT DO THAT. Why? The only thing that makes sense is the sense of responsibility that I needed to be home while she was learning. Rationally this makes no sense. She takes up a lot of space and energy. She is a teenager! Let's just say, I am glad she returned to in-person school.

STEP 2: Upgrade Your Energy

There are many things you can do to upgrade your energy. Check all the things that may help YOU recharge your energy:

- ☐ Hiking in the woods
- ☐ Taking a walk
- ☐ Jogging
- ☐ Working out
- ☐ Beach/mountain trip
- ☐ Pool/hot tub
- ☐ Taking a nap
- ☐ Taking a drive

- ☐ A night or weekend away just you
- ☐ Spa treatments – massage, hair, nails, facial
- ☐ Exercise
- ☐ Stretching
- ☐ Visualization
- ☐ Journaling
- ☐ Reading
- ☐ Creating a space just for you
- ☐ Decluttering/organizing
- ☐ Meeting up with a friend
- ☐ Talking to a friend
- ☐ Doing some yoga
- ☐ Gardening
- ☐ Mowing the lawn
- ☐ Walking barefoot
- ☐ Quiet minutes
- ☐ Going outside and enjoying the sun
- ☐ Taking a bath
- ☐ Cooking
- ☐ Energy healing
- ☐ Reiki
- ☐ Sound therapy
- ☐ Soundcodes
- ☐ Mindful breathing
- ☐ Watching a good movie/show
- ☐ Meditating/ Meditation
- ☐ Using your creativity without judgment – painting, drawing, dancing

Don't feel like you have to do everything on this list to upgrade your energy. I recommend picking what really recharges you and make them a part of your energy design, as we move through the next couple of steps.

After you've identified some activities that you think or know will rejuvenate your energy, it's time to create your Mini-Charge and Full-Charge Energy Designs. Activities that are 1-15 minutes belong on the Mini-Charge Energy Design and activities more than 15 minutes belong on the Full-Charge Energy Design. There are moments you will be short on time and will need an activity off your Mini-Charge Design. Knowing what will center, ground and uplift your energy temporarily to get you through until you can take the necessary time to completely re-charge with an activity off your Full-Charge Design is really helpful to stay at the "sustainable" level.

Energy Designs

Examples of a Mini-Charge (1-15 minutes)

- Stretching/moving your body
- Give yourself 1+ minutes to take deep breaths (this can quickly shift your energy)
- Go outside to get fresh air or soak in the sun
- Get a chair or foot massage to use regularly
- Write in your journal

Examples of a Full-Charge (15 minutes+)

- Take a bath
- Go for a walk
- Talk to a good friend
- Write in your journal
- Guided meditation

Think about things that have worked for you in a pinch and then write a list of activities for your Mini-Charge Energy Design:

Now think about things that have worked for you to fully rejuvenate and then write a list of activities for your Full-Charge Energy Design:

If this exercise is hard or nothing is coming to you, then I'd suggest making a list of activities you want to try out or try again and evaluate how you feel. This could be a great way to try something new and see if it works to recharge your energy.

STEP 3: Radiant Energy Plan

Your Radiant Energy Plan takes what you have completed in Step 1 and Step 2 and puts it into implementation mode. You have identified these activities that you know recharge you or you are going to try, now it's time to take this and embody it in your day-to-day life. Setting yourself up to feel good in your energy, in either "sustaining" or "thriving," as defined earlier in this chapter. Having a plan without implementation doesn't do you any good, right? You want to feel radiant.

There are proactive tasks that I recommend to jumpstart your Radiant Energy Plan. One is to create a special space just for you. This doesn't need to be elaborate or your own room. I have a client who used her master walk-in closet to set up her own space to retreat to, even if it was for only 10 minutes.

For me personally, I was using my office as a space to retreat to. Over time I realized it wasn't as relaxing as I had imagined it to be. Too much "biz energy" in the space for me to expand enough, so I designated a space just for me in my bedroom. I bought a chair and a small table to use for my books and crystals, along with a great footstool, chair and foot massager. It helped me get the relaxing and retreat vibes I was looking for in my "me space." I also have face and lip masks to use when I want to have a spa vibe.

Think about what space you can have just for you. Where is it? Then go set it up!

Have your Mini-Charge Energy Design on a sheet, maybe laminated, hanging in your office or in a place where you can easily access it when needed. Alternatively, have it in a document on your computer or in the notes section of your phone. Of course, there is the option to have them in all the places! Since I am still into the paper planner, I have a list in the beginning of my planner with my Mini-Charge activities.

Get out your calendar, planner, phone, or whatever you use to schedule your time. Plan ahead to schedule yourself into your calendar. Those activities on your Full-Charge Energy Design, pick one and schedule it in. You can figure out for your own energy, what does that look like weekly, monthly, and quarterly. Having regular dates with yourself will help keep you in "sustaining" and "thriving" energy.

The last thing any of us need is to burnout. This takes a toll on our emotional, mental and physical health. It could take double, triple, quadruple or more time to completely come back from burning out. If you have experienced a burnout, you are aware of the toll it takes on us, especially as introverts.

At this time, I will also point out that those Mini-Charges are good when you only have a short timeframe, but they are not designed to rejuvenate in a way that brings us to "sustainable" and "thriving" long-term.

Think about your cell phone, when you are in the red and do a quick charge, it doesn't take long before you are back in the red. It happens faster than you think. Keep your awareness on your energy to avoid burn out and get yourself to "thriving" energy. When you start doing these steps, it will become apparent how great you feel on such a deep level. Strive to have "Thriving" energy. Take a minute and think about how often you need a Full-Charge. Make that a priority in your calendar.

Speaking of your calendar, a great habit to implement is creating more white space and buffers in your calendar. Don't overbook yourself in a way that doesn't feel good. You know what works best for you, but you may not have implemented it. Take the time now to create that space for yourself in between appointments. Don't forget this is for both personal and business.

If this is a new concept for you or it is not something that you've done before, give it a try. If you are using an appointment scheduler, creating buffer/white space is easy to do in the settings of the system. This is a time for implementation and shift when things aren't working well for you.

We are always learning and our lives change. Something that worked three months ago, might not work today. Always be aware of when your energy feels drained and is leaking, especially when it comes to your appointments, meetings, and obligations.

Then there is scheduling the fun times with family, friends, etc. Although these may show up on your rejuvenation "me time," there are times when we forget to schedule in fun time. Am I the only one guilty of this?

Quick review of Step 3 Radiant Energy Plan Implementation:

1. Create Your Special Space.

2. Easy Access to Your Mini-Charge Energy Design.

3. Plan Rejuvenation with Your Full-Charge Energy Design.

4. Add White/Buffer Space in Your Day (personal and business).

5. Add "FUN" into your calendar.

STEP 4: Evaluate Your Energy

Evaluating your energy is an ongoing habit to add to your daily life. When you are aware of your energy, it will ensure you're consistently pinpointing energy leaks and upgrading your energy, especially important for us introverts.

I recommend having the "Daily Energy Evaluation Tool" available throughout your day. Print out a few and rate your energy every day for a week or two and see if there are any consistent energy leaks, what recharges your energy, and then decide to make any shifts that will keep your energy at "sustainable" or "thriving" level.

It's not about minute-for-minute energy exchange. What I mean by this is although there was a 3-hour meeting you attended, it doesn't necessarily mean you need to recoup for three hours. For you it could mean you need more time or even less time. Pay close attention as you evaluate your energy.

Overall Energy Evaluation Tool

Rate your current energy level (1-5):
1= Exhausted and need to retreat to bed
3= You need a little boost of energy
5= Excited and energized to move to the next thing

1 2 3 4 5

Brain dump all the things you're currently doing on a daily/weekly basis.

Circle what's depleting your energy. What actions or boundaries can be put in place to better support your energy?

What are 3-5 things you can intentionally choose from your Mini-Charge or Full-Charge to bring up your energy level.

-
-
-
-
-

Did anything on this list not deplete my energy, but increased it?

Daily Energy Evaluation Tool

Rate your current energy level (1-5):
1= Exhausted and need to retreat to bed
3= You need a little boost of energy
5= Excited and energized to move to the next thing

What was your rating earlier?
1 2 3 4 5

What is your rating now?
1 2 3 4 5

What are you doing or what did you finish doing?

Depending on your rating, did it deplete your energy? Did it increase your energy?

If what you did depleted your energy, identify an activity on your Mini-Charge or Full-Charge Energy Designs you can do to increase your energy?

The Energy Evaluation Tool gets you to look deeper into your own energy patterns, how it is affected by other people and situations and what it takes to get you back to "thriving."

Your Best Energy

Realizing what time you are at your best will help align your day with your natural patterns. If you have the majority of your energy in the morning, then I encourage you to plan your day around those times. The high energy tasks get scheduled for the morning. Knowing your high energy time will guide you to make better decisions when scheduling appointments (business and personal), networking, projects, client interactions, calls, etc.

In tracking our energy, we may discover that some activities we thought were amping up our energy are actually depleting! Here's an example of an activity I thought rejuvenated me but I realized didn't: watching tv shows. Although I'm not doing much when I am watching them, watching them is not rejuvenating. I'm always under the impression that this will get me to relax and rejuvenate my energy. In the end, I am just as tired or more tired after watching a movie or show. I'm an adrenaline junky so anything that keeps me going in a show (and of course I am a binger) I just get sucked in. If you find yourself in my shoes, it can be helpful to set some healthy habits around watching tv shows. Get curious about the activities you do that you assume are rejuvenating.

Constant and consistent awareness of your energy is key to not getting to the point of needing so much rejuvenation you can't function day-to-day, or you are just getting by. Starting a habit where you keep a journal of your energy level, what triggered the increase or decrease in energy or use the Energy Evaluation Tool. You may be surprised that what you thought was bringing you energy might actually not be helping at all. Sometimes things work the way you want them to, others do not, and frankly, things shift—so what could have brought you energy last year, isn't cutting it this year. Giving you the tools to really hone in on a daily basis on what your energy is like throughout the day, month, quarter, and year is really important. Using these tools will help you see shifts quicker so you can make adjustments and not end up needing a month off from life! I know, I know, we all dream about it at some point. Let's not forget the replenishment of your energy isn't always minute for minute and sometimes, a full rejuvenation won't actually take a month.

Chapter 6

Being a Mom / Introvert / Entrepreneur

During the process of writing this book, I felt led to speak to the mom Intropreneurs that are reading this book and share some thoughts about being a wife, mom and entrepreneur.

Taking care of our family is very much a top priority and so is taking care of ourselves. It can be a hard task to take care of ourselves at times, especially when our kids are really little or when they are demanding of our time. Take what you learned in the last chapter (The Introvert's Energy Toolkit), and apply it to your other roles in life, including being a mom, a wife, etc.

This past summer, I found myself deciding to push the "slow mo" button. I wasn't taking a full pause, but I made a conscious decision to shift more of my time and energy to my family responsibilities. This made me happy and I enjoyed summer life with the kiddos. I continued some of my house projects that were started in the late spring. I felt content when I woke up in the morning, planned activities, and really enjoyed some downtime. This also gave me the time for me to workout, read, journal, do a gratitude practice, etc. My life felt fulfilled throughout the summer, even though I pushed the "slow mo" button.

When I decided to look at pushing the "slow-mo" button with a lens of love and opportunity to have more dedicated family/kid time, I was able to have gratitude for the time. What I decided to do was put my business on auto-pilot, less planned growth, more of a knowing/my intuition telling me this was the right direction for me in the moment. If I could work 1-2 hours a week, it would sustain my business. Getting down to the bare minimum of what needed to be accomplished, figuring out the things that I could delegate, and recognizing what could be done in the future made the pause/slow-mo easier to accept.

Being a recovering perfectionist and workaholic, this process brought up some negative thinking. Thoughts like: *You have to be working more or you aren't going to make any money. You need to be out there meeting new people or your business won't have a pipeline.* This inner saboteur was chatting in my head. Once I was able to settle into the space of increased family responsibilities, I was able to embrace the situation and be in love with exactly where I was in my life.

How to prepare for a "pause" or "slow-mo" button being pushed:

- Prepare your business for when you may need to shift your attention away or spend less time on your business.

- Use your Mini-Charge Energy Design to find those little pieces of time to recharge quickly.

- Mentally prepare for a shift. Although it may not happen immediately, when you are mentally prepared for a shift to happen, it takes less energy.

Spending extended time alone, maybe a full weekend, really does make me a better business owner, mom, wife, and friend. I will say it is easier now that my kids are a bit older. So if you are a mom of small children, it takes a different tactic to get that time in. Here are some suggestions: hire a high school sitter for a couple of hours after school once, twice, or three times a month, whatever feels right to you. If your children are not in school yet, maybe having them in daycare or with a nanny 1-2x a week could help out. If family lives close by, having your kids visit with relatives may be an option.

This last year brought many realizations. Laying down for a few hours was a way that would rejuvenate me in the past. Recently, I've been trying this and it no longer works the way it had before. I had to make some shifts and a bit of trial and error to figure out what would work for me now.

The first half of 2021, I kept telling my family and anyone who would listen, that I needed a month away from everyone and everything. I was convinced this would rejuvenate me to "thriving." I've never actually done this, so how do I know that would even work? Well I don't! It felt good talking about it. The feelings that came up when I imagined being alone were relief, calmness, contentment. I imagined I'd have time to contemplate life, and not be rushed to the next thing on the list. It felt like a glorious time to take care of me and not have any responsibility for anyone else. I never did try it out. Honestly, I'm not sure I would last being away from my family that long but it sure felt good to imagine not feeling overwhelmed by life and the only responsibility would be myself.

Instead of dreaming about all the goodness that a month away would be, I decided to go away for the weekend and get in all the month-long vibes. It helped but honestly it brought me to "sustaining" and my energy dipped fairly quickly shortly thereafter, once I was back into the responsibilities of my life. After that, I became hyper-aware of what would rejuvenate me on a daily basis. I took my own advice from the last chapter and completed the Daily Energy Evaluation every day for two weeks. What an eye-opener!

There are tools that helped me move through to the other side, when I just couldn't seem to keep my energy charged. I was allowing all my life and business responsibilities to cloud my thinking. To gain some clarity here are some tools that I used (and continue to), and hope they are helpful to you in your life.

Tool: Brain Dump

Brain Dumping is a tool used when starting something new or if you feel like your brain can't handle one more thing. When you feel overwhelmed and you couldn't possibly add one more thing to the list. Here's how I use this tool:

1. Take three deep breaths before getting started.

2. Set a 2-minute timer and write as much as you can.

3. Make two columns on your paper personal and business or make one big list, whatever feels best for you.

4. Write everything that is in your brain.

5. Add another 2 minutes to your timer, if you have more to write.

6. Go through your list(s) and categorize the list using the 4 D's of time management: Do (things that need to get done in the new future), Delay (things you want to do but can wait), Delegate (things that you can delegate to someone else), Delete (things that you want to not do at all).[4]

7. Take your Do List and prioritize each item from most important to least.

8. Create an Action Plan for your Do List.

How do you feel after this exercise?

When my clients do this exercise they feel a weight lifted and a feeling of coming out of the cloud of chaos. Keeping track of all of our responsibilities, including the what, when, who and how it will all get done, takes up a lot of mental energy. This exercise brings forth all the things in our brains in the moment and frees up energy once it is on paper and out of our brain. In addition, it can lead to

---

[4] Jack Canfield, *The Power of Focus.*

improved focus, priorities, and less distractions.

Tool: Morning Routine

We hear all the time that having a morning routine helps start your day right. I couldn't agree more. I feel good when I have at least 10-15 minutes of "grounding" time before getting the day started. How about you?

Although my practice has ranged from 15 minutes to 2 hours, depending on the day and what I need in that particular moment of my life. A morning routine has really made a difference in not only grounding me for the day, but giving me clarity. I've used the Miracle Morning[5] over the years, which I've adapted to my own morning routine. The most fulfilling has been my most recent morning practice, where I have incorporated a couple different practices, including Morning Mastermind Meditation by Boni Lonnsbury[6] and the Generosity Practice that was created by Christina Frei.[7] It takes about 20 minutes and my practice feels grounding, productive and most importantly BEING present in the present moment. I keep a notepad close by for those thoughts that come in or things needing to go on the to-do list. Then I can jot them down and get back to being present without those distracting thoughts.

Do you have a morning routine? What's working for you and what are the benefits of your morning routine?

---

[5] Hal Elrod, *Miracle Morning.*
[6] https://livealifeyoulove.com/?s=morning+mastermind
[7] Christina Frei, *The Generosity Practice: 40 Days to Unstoppable.*

The Importance of Delegation

As an introvert entrepreneur, I have realized I don't have to do it all. I can delegate tasks. Taking a look at what your needs are, how you can delegate tasks, and how much it will cost (in some cases, there will be no cost depending on who is in your household). Some of the most sought after help is house cleaning, childcare, lawn maintenance, and meal prep/cooking. If you have a spouse, they may be willing to take on some tasks that traditionally you did. You can keep costs low for the delegated tasks, perhaps a high school student can come and help around the house or do the lawn. Think about what could free up some of your time and energy, so you can focus on your family and business. Even if you are just starting out, there are still tasks that can be delegated.

Tool: Shifting from DOING to BEING

BEING has been a real challenge for me, so finding ways to shift from DOING to BEING has proved a powerful tool in my life and business. Every time I feel like I've embraced BEING, something comes up that makes me question am I truly BEING in the moment? Am I truly present?

How do you really know? My final answer is you'll know! When I am in a state of BEING, I am calm, not worried, grounded in the life I've created. I see everything through the rose-colored glasses. In the present time I'm not getting caught up in my thoughts, my mind doesn't wander to the future nor the past. I take in the scenery, take in a few extra breaths, and really enjoy the time right there in front of me.

As I was creating a practice of being more present in my life, the book *The Power of Now* by Ekhart Tolle was recommended to me. This book made an impact and helped me to practice not being worried about the future or allowing the past to be just that, the past.

BEING in the moment does take effort and the ability to shift, if you find yourself somewhere else. What I have noticed in my own life, is that there are moments that I pass up to stick with my idea of what's next. I'll give you a quick example. I had it in my mind to workout when I got home. My youngest asked me to do a project with him with glue and paper. I initially said no. I had to workout! As I said those words, it reminded me that I am passing my life away waiting to do the next thing on my to-do list. I paused and thought, 'make memories in the moment."

Delaying my workout for 10 minutes wasn't the end of the world. In fact, the project my youngest wanted to do was quick, easy and I was able to fill his heart with love and attention. In turn, it filled my heart and I felt good getting my workout done after helping him. Savoring these moments as a mom can get jumbled in all the responsibilities and our own self-care. Stay in the moment and shift whenever possible to practice BEING present.

Intropreneur in Action

Nancy's Story

"Coming from a family of divorce, at a time when it was not common, I often felt like an outsider when trying to fit in. Also being more of an introvert, my alone time has always been an important way for me to recharge, especially after being around large groups of people.

When I sold my yoga and wellness center and began working more from home a few years ago, I realized I had a strong desire to develop more meaningful relationships. At the same time, I also realized that I had developed a story that said, "Connecting with new people is awkward and draining."

And yet looking back, I have developed many wonderful relationships over the years....one-to-one, just the way I like it.

So I decided to create a new story/belief that says, 'Creating new relationships is fun and nourishing in new and unexpected ways. I love meeting new people.' I also know that I can set boundaries that work for me. Since I made that decision, I have a new perspective and the reward has been connecting with some wonderful new people."

-3-

Growing Your Business

Chapter 7

Go Deep Not Wide

Over the years, I have witnessed in my real estate business that relationships matter. Not keeping your business and your personal life separate can actually make for a "whole" person and fulfilled life. It's part of the lifestyle. We can be our authentic self. There's no fake it til you make it. I can be my full self. The authentic me. The people in my circle know me and want to be in my circle and my energy.

Being in business as an introvert can have its challenges. One thing that is true for most introverts is we have deep relationships with people and we care deeply, as demonstrated in the earlier chapter talking about introverted gifts. This is where you can shine. Whether you are just starting out or you want to grow your business, cultivating and nurturing deep relationships is the path to creating your own success (whatever that looks like for you).

Who is part of your circle? That is your decision. You can choose who is in your circle. You can be the one to build relationships that matter with the people that reflect your greater purpose. When you look at who is already in your circle, think about the characteristics of the people. Do you value particular character traits like those who are trustworthy, helpful, giving, fun, supportive, introspective, open thinking? What are the top three characteristics of your current circle of people?

Remember those top characteristics when you meet new people and are considering adding them to your circle. Always be open to inviting people that would benefit from being part of your circle. You are always open to inviting more like-minded people into your circle.

When you connect with someone, how do you know they have values or characteristics that you are looking for? Ultimately, you have to get to know them! Building and nurturing relationships does take time, these things do not happen overnight. The following questions will help you to get to know others.

Connecting Questions

1. "Tell me a little bit about yourself."

2. "What hobbies do you have?"

3. "I'm reading _____. Have you read it? This is what I've gotten out of it so far, how about you?" If they haven't read it, give them a quick summary.

4. If they have a business: "What are you most passionate about in your business?"

5. "How can I help or support you?"

If you meet up with someone who is not aligned or they seem a little off but you're not sure what it is... when you get that gut feeling, something is off. Trust your gut. Trust your intuition. That person may not be a terrible person, but if it doesn't feel right, they are not someone to invite into your circle.

When you are moving through the process of growing your circle, keep your values, mission, and passion in mind as you are meeting people. Having this at the forefront of your mind will help you weed out the people who are not aligned with you and are not meant to be part of your circle.

Friendships are such an important part of your circle and your community. Creating and nurturing your community of people sets you up for growing your business while nourishing your soul and other people. Over the years, I have met so many women just by showing up and interacting with them. Many of the ones that ended up in my circle over a decade ago are still part of my life and business.

Building a few deep connections rather than many shallow relationships will fill you up. These are the people who will encourage you when you're struggling. They will help you plant the seeds and grow your business by being your biggest cheerleader. They will turn to you when they need encouragement, referrals and refer people to you. These relationships are mutually beneficial. You have heard of win-win. Well, this is win-win-win because everyone benefits! Everyone is elevated by the connection and relationship.

Do you value connections, relationships, referrals, working together, elevating one another, win-win-win scenarios?

This way of doing business has shown me that going deep in my relationships and connections with people conserves my energy, reaps more business, more income, and I get to spend the most time with the people I care about and want to give value to.

The concept of Go Deep, Not Wide was created to teach and guide people to grow a referral-based business. Here's the concept. Going wide is always hustling to meet as many new people as possible and growing a large or wide list of connections. This isn't necessarily bad, but it does set you up for lots of shallow relationships, depleted energy, and increased expenses (more on this in a later chapter).

For an introvert, having a lot of shallow-level relationships is not energy-giving, it is energy-draining because we thrive in deeper relationships with people. There is only so much energy that you can give as an introvert. Spending our time wisely, like with the people in our circle, not only conserves our energy but in some cases may even increase an introvert's energy.

It's so important to have people around you that lift you up and that you can lift up too.

Surround yourself with the most amazing people that

totally get you, your business, and want to support you in every way including blossoming friendships. These people have missions and visions that help and support their clients, their community and their message is spreading throughout the world. It's an opportunity to link arms with other introverted women entrepreneurs on their journey and be there to support each other.

Connect with people regularly (at least quarterly, if not monthly for those Master Connectors). I would be hard pressed to say you need to connect with everyone 1:1 every, single month. That makes me drained just thinking about it! What I will say is if you want to nurture your relationships, identify the people that stand out as Master Connectors. These are people where you felt an immediate connection with, maybe you talked about partnering on a project, you have similar interests, your businesses compliment each other, or they've given you multiple referrals, are one of your biggest cheerleaders, whatever the reason, your Master Connectors are the key to growing and sustaining your business. These people are usually in your life not just for business, but personally too. They enhance your personal life. They are someone you could pick up the phone and call or text, someone that would listen if you had a bad day and needed some moral support. The best part is it is mutual, you care about them and are there when they need a friend.

Relationships take time! I am not saying you need to have 1,000 people in your circle. How could you possibly connect with all of them? I am all about quality over quantity. This is the overall concept of Go Deep, Not Wide. Focus on the potent few, maybe you start by making a list of 25 people you know, if you are just starting out. If you have an established business and you have a 1000+ people on your list, it is time to start sorting through those relationships. Make a list of 25 Master Connectors. These are the people who see the value in you, your service/product, and want to help you in any way possible.

Master Connectors are the people you are most connected to, have deep relationships with, and the people you want to spend the majority of your time with giving back and adding value.

One strong referral partner is better than 50 biz cards of people you don't really know. We can reject the cultural norm, that we, as introverts, need to conform to the extroverted world. We do not need to meet as many people as possible and add them to your circle. Our success is not reliant on having a large quantity of contacts in a "little black book." As an introvert, this probably makes you want to curl up and be left alone! Or at least that's my reaction to this cultural norm.

It is up to us as individuals to realize who we are, at our core, our authentic self, and use that to create the life and business we want. It also molds our circle of people we want to interact with, spend time with, give back to, and ultimately create a community of people who are exactly who you want to interact with on a daily, monthly, yearly basis.

Your Circle

When teaching about building your circle of

connections, I ask everyone to imagine a target, like a bullseye. It is a great way to show the process of a connection to move through the three layers.

Organizing your connections allows you to prioritize your time spent with them. There are people in the smallest part of the bullseye, these are the people who have already described earlier, your Master Connectors. These are the ones you can call upon to get the word out about your products/services, share upcoming events, whether we ask them or not! They will be the first to refer you to their family, friends, acquaintances, and their circle of people.

Master Connectors are your smallest circle and most potent of friends and business partners. They are the ones that you can count on to spread the word on anything you have going on. They are your biggest cheerleader.

The next layer out are Second Connectors. These are the middle circle of people who are just starting to interact, maybe sending referrals, sharing, contributing in some way to the group as a whole.

The outer and last layer are your Third Connectors, these are the people who have just come into your circle, they have been outliers for a bit, or they support you but haven't had the opportunity to support you in an outwardly way, for example referrals, sharing your information. Typically these people will move from here to Second Connectors and then to Master Connectors or they find themselves outside the circle.

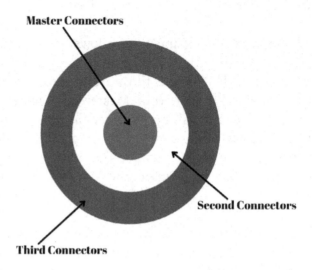

Your list of Master Connectors are the people you want to spend the most time with. You want them to feel valued. Their friendships matter to you and you want them to enjoy being part of the circle. We talk more in Chapter 12 about how to add value, celebrate them, and have them feel special.

How to Deepen Your Connections

I suggest that you go into your relationships with no expectation of anything in return. It really detaches from the expectation of "getting" something from someone and the connections go deeper. Using questions to get to know people better both personally and professionally. Asking questions are important. One of an introvert's greatest gifts, as you read earlier, is listening. Using this gift during in-person events, while connecting with even one person shows your interest in the person. If it goes well, then you should make sure you ask for the best contact information and schedule a 1:1. These 1:1 meetings are part of getting to know people on a deeper level.

When you have 1:1 time with someone, it is a perfect opportunity to collect personal and business information. These details will help you get to know the person better and be able to customize your connection with that person. For example: If you both have children of the same age – you can connect on a personal level through that.

When you listen, take notes. This gives you the opportunity to remember and reinforce the information. Taking notes keeps you engaged. I've created a great tool for this called the Intropreneur Connection Journal.[8] This journal is a key to recording information and really getting to know people. It also allows you some reflection after the conversation. Things like what attracted you to the person you are connecting with. There are little reminders like, *'How can I help and support you? Who can I connect this person with?'* You want to be in the mode of giving when having conversations.

In the end, we want joyful connections. All of the

---

[8] Access the Intropreneur Connection Journal at:
https://bit.ly/intropreneurconnectionjournal

people in your circle should bring you joy. Remember when you are connecting with someone 1:1, you want it to feel exciting and joyful. That's when you really know this is the right person to have or bring into your circle.

Chapter 8

Love Up Your Community

Loving up on your people puts a smile on their face, fills your heart with gratitude, and keeps you top of mind. You are probably thinking, "well, how do I love up on them?" Start by asking yourself, "how do I want them to feel being part of my community?" In my experience and those of my clients, we want people to feel cared for, loved, seen, heard, and valued.

Love on the people you know by taking what brings you joy in your business and look for opportunities to love on the people in your circle. When you do this, they will want to support you and your business!

One way to stay in touch, top of mind, and show you care is by sending a personal note, a little something I like to call "Love Mail." Everyone loves "Love Mail." I always have note cards and stamps ready to send out, along with a little something extra. This could be a journal, book, inspirational card, etc. Think about something you would want to get in the mail to put a smile on your face. When you meet people, you can ask for their mailing address, if it is not on their business card or promotional material. You can also ask for their mailing address when you follow up with them via email or private message. I haven't had one person not give me their address. Giving love mail is such a gift of gratitude.

When deciding how to grow, give back, and add value to your community, consider the things that bring you joy and excitement. Clients have started in-person and Zoom Coffee Connections and it has been a great way to bring people together in their community. Not only to meet each other but a place to get to know them better. Out of wanting to connect with others and your need to bring value into their lives, you bring them together. Maybe there is a common thread, it could be business, but it also can be hobbies, kids, dogs, anything that could bring your people together. This looks different for everyone, so find what you love to do for people and how you like to bring people together and use that as a stepping stone to love up on your community.

Hosting client appreciation events is one of my most favorite things to do. It gives people in my community a chance to meet each other, have their kiddos play together (when events are specific to kids), give back to the community, and an opportunity to have sponsors advertise their businesses.

Also keep in mind, as you build your community, ask them what they want. It gives them some ownership in the community to interact and give value. A great way to do this is to have surveys via email, talk to people 1:1, or do a poll in a Facebook group. Gathering feedback from the people really makes an impact and people want to be part of grassroots initiatives and engagement/attendance increases.

Ideas for Adding Value to Your Community Throughout the Year

- Small thoughtful gifts.

- Events such as Connecting events (Coffee Connections), Networking events (Speed Networking), Masterminds, Speaker events (live videos, guests in Facebook groups, or podcast guests).

- Client appreciation i.e. Community Appreciation events (in person or online).

- Contests! Encourages engagement, fun and free stuff.

- Personal handwritten notes.

- Social media - Facebook group with tips, special learning on subjects, opportunity to share social events.

- Giving Back on a bigger scale - Look into your heart for a cause that is near and dear to you and put together a way you can give back on a bigger/larger scale.

- Emails & Newsletters - A way to stay connected digitally or with snail mail on topics/tips that you think your community would find helpful.

Every quarter bring your Master Connectors together, give a little extra gratitude and time with these people who have been your biggest cheerleaders. Letting them know how much you value their friendship, support and referrals. Master Connectors are the ones who have given you the most referrals, repeat business, and biggest business shoutouts whenever they have the opportunity. They are really committed to your business success, so why not love on them more than the rest of your community?

Plan out your year to stay consistent and top of mind! Action and implementation are important when it comes to loving up on your community.

Plan Out Your Year

1. What do you do now to Love on Your Community?

2. What do you want to start doing to Love on Your Community?

3. What activities will you do monthly, quarterly, and yearly?

- Monthly:

- Quarterly:

- Yearly:

Red Carpet Experience

Have you thought about your client/customer red carpet experience before, during and after they purchase from you? Focusing on your clients reaps referrals, repeat business, and increased income. Taking everything you have learned and contemplated about loving on your community, think about how you want your clients and customers to feel during their experience. What do you do for your clients when they decide to purchase from you? Here are some ideas...

- Send a note, gift, or email with a personalized thank you!

- Questionnaire asking "get to know you" questions.

- Offer a loyalty program.

- Say thank you for referrals and repeat biz with a note or gift.

- Ask for testimonials.

- Support them in a way that aligns with your business and the service/product you provide.

Chapter 9

Introverts are *Good* at Networking

Being intentional when networking and connecting is important, whether online or in-person.

When everything went online with no in-person networking throughout most of the United States and around the world in the Spring of 2020, I thought that I had to network everywhere that was offering online opportunities, simply because I could. I burnt myself out over that summer, going to all of those network events.

You want to always be inviting new people into your circle. Networking can help you do just that. I'm not suggesting hundreds of people. You decide what inviting new people in looks like for you. Personally I go through these sprints where I want to meet a few more people than usual. I'll schedule one or two extra networking events every few months.

Always be on the lookout for new places to meet people that fit your "circle." The best way to find these new places is to ask for referrals. You have a great circle of people and some of them are business owners, so always be asking where people are networking and connecting. More often than not, the places your people are networking and connecting, are the same place you will find your people.

It's a process to figure out if the places you connect and network with people are right for you. The best way to evaluate is to attend an event/meeting and when you are there interacting with people, listening, observing, and learning more, it will become clear if it is the right place for you. Using your intuition will be valuable during this process and throughout meeting and cultivating relationships.

Networking and connecting is not about shaking everyone's hand or messaging everyone who was on the zoom call event/meeting/mastermind. It's not about making sure that your information gets into the hands of every single person on the call or in the room.

Networking is an important part of your business, if you choose to have it part of your plan. It gives us the opportunity to meet new people that have similar values, mission, and vision. They are authentic, real people, women who are like you. For me it's finding those women who are striving towards a balance of feminine and masculine energies.

Don't feel like you aren't good enough or fun enough because you didn't walk out (or leave zoom) with a pile of biz cards (digital or otherwise). Don't ever feel like the event wasn't a success because you didn't make a connection with a bunch of people. Shift your mindset to remember that you have talents and gifts that make you shine in a very different way.

When you are sending energy out with excitement and it's truly genuine, the right people actually come to you and you can have a great conversation. Don't get me wrong, occasionally there are some not so great people who come to you, but most of the time it's really great to connect with people that you attract to yourself.

When I asked introverted entrepreneurs in my group what their biggest struggles are, networking was at the top. Three answers stuck out to me: 1) Being vulnerable, 2) Talking about myself, and 3) It's energy draining. Wow! I have those times, even now, and I consider myself a Master Connector!

When you have the opportunity to talk about yourself or about your business, do you? You might think people don't want to hear you talk about yourself, but they do! They are seeking the same things you are: connection, building their network, elevating others and themselves, and growing their business with ideal clients and income.

It can be very draining to network and connect, especially for an introvert. This is where intentional connection is important. Networking is not about shaking every hand or pitching your business to every person there. You can be selective in who you take time with.

Think about WHY you are connecting with people. Maybe something is birthed out of that connection. Maybe you are looking for a partner, or partners, to help market one of your programs. Maybe you could do the same for them. Maybe you are looking for an accountability partner and you meet someone who seems like a great match.

Whatever your intention is, bring that into your visualization. Manifest that person. Manifest an amazing meeting. Visualize it and it will come to fruition.

Finding the right places to meet and build powerful, sustainable, amazingly beautiful relationships. I mean business and personal relationships. We build connections with personal stories, stories like why you started your business and what impact you want to have in the world.

You may think your life isn't exciting or even intriguing, but people want to know who you are on a personal and professional level. It's more than just what your business is. People want to be around your energy, they know, like and trust you. Allowing people to hear your story makes an imprint on their heart.

You are going to connect. You are going to elevate. It's going to be a perfect opportunity for you to grow your business by referrals, repeat business, and bring in new people to your circle. When we set intentions for the way we network and connect, it brings us into focus as to what is really important, deep relationships.

So what are your intentions? You can set an overall intention for your business and for networking and connecting. I also recommend setting an intention for each event or meeting you attend. My overall intention, and of my clients and business circle, is to meet ONE person who I connect with at each event I attend. That might look like a private message to them to connect or get their email address to follow up later or, I write down their name to connect afterwards, if I already know we are connected via social or email.

What is your overall intention? What is your intention for when you go into a networking event or meeting, even if it is 1:1 meeting?

Intentional Networking and Connecting

Here are a few examples of overall intentions and specific intentions to get you started, use them if they feel right for you or create your own.

- I intend to be more intentional when networking and connecting.

- I intend to learn more about being intentional when I am networking and connecting.

- I intend to talk/connect with one amazing person.

- I intend to connect with one person to collaborate with on my next project/program.

- I intend to connect with one person to add to my soul circle.

- I intend to arrive early to online networking and connecting events/meetings.

- I intend to private message one person to connect with 1:1.

- I intend to have my digital business card ready to share with attendees.

- I intend to attend two networking events and connect with the leader/host.

- I intend to connect with one person that is on my list.

- I intend to create time before the networking event/meeting to gather my thoughts, focus, get grounded and be "energy" ready.

Networking Vs. Connecting

What is networking and connecting? There are many people who interchange these two words for many reasons. In the past, I used connecting in place of networking because networking was an icky, pushy, sales word for me. Today, I use them separately after realizing you need both to grow your business, your circle and your friendships. They have two very powerful meanings.

Networking: Action or process of interacting with others to exchange information and develop professional or social contacts.

Connecting: To form a relationship.

So, yes, you could just do the connecting part. But we

can take a quantum leap when you put the networking and connection together. You'll see your business is going to expand to new heights. This is where you as an Intropreneur get to make the decision what that looks like for you!

When I started talking to people in my circle and clients, here's what was being said:

"Jen, I hate networking!"

"I don't network like the others."

"I don't network like an extrovert."

"I'm not good at networking."

"I'm bothering people with my services and products when I talk about them."

"I'd rather listen to what other people are doing."

"I'd rather listen to what their dreams are rather than sharing mine."

Some of us have a habit of telling ourselves negative things that are not necessarily true. But they have collected evidence to support these negative thoughts. I'm guilty of it!

When we believe something is true our subconscious gets on board. We see things that validate what we are thinking. If we make some shifts in what we believe and our networking story, we can eliminate these negative thoughts.

When you reframe your thinking, it shifts your posture. It shifts your thoughts on networking.

What we believe is usually because of a negative experience you had at some point or you have heard other people's negative stories.

2020 gave us perspective. Getting online to network and meet people has been a blessing... mostly! It can be overwhelming and lead to burnout if we're not careful, but it does give introverts an opportunity to show up and be seen.

That can be really difficult or really exciting. The good news is, you get to decide. You get to frame your thoughts and make this a negative or a positive.

If you find yourself having negative thoughts around networking, how can you reframe them?

Write down one belief that comes to mind and then we will work on reframing it together.

Start by writing down your limiting beliefs. They might look something like this:

I don't like to network.

I'm not good at networking.

I don't want to share my story.

I feel spammy when I talk about my product or services.

Now we are going to take that thought and turn it around. We are going to CHOOSE to believe the positive instead of the negative.

Examples:

I don't like to network = I love to connect with others. (Remember the difference between networking and connecting?)

I am bad at networking = I'm good at networking or I'm okay at networking. Note: It's ok if you're not already great at it, but choose to believe that you are not bad at it and that you can continue to improve.

I feel spammy when I talk about my product or services = I don't network to sell to people, I network to connect with people and build deep relationships.

Find the evidence that says you are a good connector and networker. If you can't find anything then I really want you to sit and believe that you are a good networker. Then take small steps to improve your networking. Join smaller networking groups so that it is less overwhelming. Find a group where you know someone who will be there, whether in person or on zoom. Bring a "wing woman" with you! It's all about using our connections to help us with certain things. In this case, use your connections to make you more comfortable in a meeting.

Even the most introverted business owner can be good at networking and connecting! Shift your beliefs. Find evidence that shows you are good at this or take that action step, that one small step that says, "I'm going to go do this and make this a positive experience!"

Walking In

I have talked before about shifting your thoughts surrounding networking and connecting and turning them into the positive. Believing you are good at networking goes a long way, but let's talk about how to feel confident walking into each meeting (or logging in on zoom, as the case may be).

Networking meetings used to be really hard for me. Sometimes they still are, but to get past that, I developed some strategies that help me.

As an introvert entrepreneur, it can be really difficult to put yourself out there. You don't want to talk about yourself. You don't want to get out of your comfort zone and make new connections. Honestly, the whole process can be draining.

People DO want to hear about me, what my passion is, my vulnerabilities. It makes me a real person. I am able to just say, "you know what? This is me!" That is so freeing, and authentic.

I use visualization to think of things that would go right. Before I walked in, I would visualize the entire meeting. I had set my intentions that I was going to meet that one person and then I would visualize how that would go.

Get there a little bit early. You get to meet the host and maybe their leadership team. You get to meet a few people on a more personal level. It might feel uncomfortable, but I tell you, when you start visualizing it will make a huge difference. It really does help your connection confidence.

Try It Yourself

Think about what your intention is for the meeting, and then visualize that happening. Picture the other people in the room and the conversations that will happen.

Here are some more tips:

- Be ready, in a one-on-one, to ask some good questions. What is their passion? What is their story? How did they get to where they are?

- Be ready to answer their questions, too. Be ready to share your story. It doesn't have to be lengthy. Your story will help people connect with you.

- Be ready to share your pitch. Have it ready so you are not caught off guard when someone asks.

- Plan to share some personal things about yourself, too. Prepare for this ahead of time. Think about things you might be comfortable sharing that will allow others to feel connected to you.

- Visualize the one-on-ones as going well. Visualize how you want it to go and what you hope will come out of it. See it happening and manifest it.

- Show up early to the meetings to start having conversations and to get comfortable with your surroundings.

- Know exactly what you have to offer.

- Know what value you bring and how you can help the people you meet.

- Always be ready to give a referral.

- Take notes during the meeting to help stay focused and to help remember key things that caught your attention. This also helps you connect during the meeting.

- Always follow up. If you connect with someone and ask for an e-mail address, make sure you email them and follow up. Do it RIGHT AWAY so you don't forget. Respond to emails quickly as well.

- Private message people. You can private message in Zoom. If you feel a connection to someone, send a message and let them know why you want to connect with them. Write down their name, try to find them on Facebook, give them a call or send an email. Don't spam people, just shoot a message to let them know you would like to connect.

Chapter 10

Re-Imagining the "Follow-Up"

You may have heard the phrase *Business is in the follow-up*. This is so true! The question then becomes, why do so many small business owners not consistently follow-up? After polling my group Connect & Elevate and my clients, this is the consensus. They think follow-up is bothering people, hard to track/automate, not sure how to follow up or what to say, are afraid people think it's only about the money and might not think that anyone would want to buy from them.

I mean why do we really need to follow up in business? Follow-up allows us to stand out from the crowd (of people who don't follow up), be top of mind with our community and clients, and stay consistently connected. The concept of following up circles back to the previous chapter talking about Loving on Your Community. All of these seem beneficial to your business, its growth, and it fills your soul because you follow up from the heart.

Now the next logical step is figuring out when you follow up? My recommendation is to follow up immediately, or within 24-48 hours. Here is a list of trigger events that will prompt you to follow up. Take note that this list is not all inclusive, but given to you as a starting point to develop your own list of when you follow up.

The why and when seem fairly straight forward. It's when entrepreneurs start getting into the how and tracking that seems to prove difficult. There are few reasons I've uncovered over the years. Many entrepreneurs are big picture visionaries and the details and the how are tasks that could be delegated to a "doer" and "implementer." What do you do if this isn't something that you can pass along to someone else? Make the process as simple and easy as possible.

When to Follow Up

- When you meet new people.

- When you are in a meeting/event and something sparks your interest and you want to touch base with that person.

- Social media interaction.

- If you receive a referral from someone.

- You want to give a referral to someone you met.

- You offered to send information or a link.

- You've seen someone you haven't talked with in awhile.

- Just because.

If you are an entrepreneur who is just starting out, you may not have a CRM system. That is ok! Go ahead and get out a spreadsheet and start adding your contacts and begin to track interactions. Seasoned entrepreneurs probably have a system to keep contacts in, along with tasks, notes, and other ways to automate the process of tracking, etc. Use its features to your advantage.

If you have a system but don't know too much about how to use it, you have a couple options: 1) utilize the help desk of your system or 2) find someone that is using the same system and see if they will help you to utilize it to meet your follow-up goals. I had a client who dedicated a portion of her Fridays to "Follow-up Friday" weekly and she invited others to join her with accountability.

You have a good idea of when to follow up with the list. Don't forget to add to it as you go along your entrepreneurial journey. Now let's look at how to do it and what to track.

Think back about what brings you joy in your business and keep that in the forefront as you go through this list of "How to Follow Up" that aligns with your authentic self and brings you joy.

Remember following up doesn't stop with one task. The end goal is to develop a relationship and nurture it, so not a one-and-done type of action. Go back or think about the times you will follow up with people and develop an action plan for each that includes "if then" prompted tasks.

How to Follow Up

- Email

- Private Message/Direct Message on social media by text, voice or video

- Text

- Handwritten Personal Note

- Call

- Invite to an event or 1:1

- Gift or Product Sample

For example, when you follow up with someone you met by sending an email with a message such as "thank you for the great conversation" you can invite them to meet 1:1 for 30 minutes. Schedule a task for 2-3 days after the email to follow up if they didn't respond to send a quick reminder note. If they respond, make sure there's a confirmation email that goes out after they schedule (preferably in your calendar link). Then automate from there with reminders. After the 1:1, set up an email task to send a follow-up email asking for their mailing address to send some love mail. You may also send an invite to your email newsletter/tips, events, and/or Facebook group (if you have one). In addition, asking how you can help and support them and follow through on their request in a timely manner.

As an entrepreneur, follow-up is one of the most important parts of making connections. If you make a connection, be sure to follow up! If you promised them a referral or a link to an article you read, be sure to follow through with it. Preparing yourself to move beyond the fear of bothering someone, I invite you to use some tools discussed earlier in this book. Ground yourself in your intention to follow up and visualize the positive outcome. Your intention to grow and nurture relationships, while using your introvert gifts and adding value to someone's life. Stay focused in the intention and all else will fall into place when it comes to the fear of bothering people.

Avoid shallow follow-up like adding someone to your email list. Don't just bombard their email box with unsolicited emails. Once you get to know someone better, you may ask them if they would like to receive your emails or newsletter. If you do this, make sure you are offering value in your newsletters.

Don't forget to ask questions. You want the other person to feel that they can share their story and their passion. Zoom one-on-ones are great for that!

Chapter 11

The Power of Online Groups

Online groups can be an amazing place to network, connect and add value to an audience that compliments your business and personality.

Online groups can also be very overwhelming because there are so many to choose from.

There are ways that you can find the right groups for you. There's no guarantee to know beforehand which are the best fit. Sometimes you just need to interact and even observe for a little bit to see what the vibe and content of the group is.

You will want to look for groups with like-minded people. This is a great opportunity to utilize our business circle and ask for referrals to groups they've enjoyed being a part of.

As you find like-minded people, decide if they are your avatar or your ideal client. Evaluate the groups that don't fit with exactly what you are looking for. Remember, you can't actively interact in every group out there! Pick and choose your top five or six groups that you want to interact with and add value. Remember to always evaluate quarterly or every six months the groups that you are in and see if the groups continue to align with you and your business.

An important part of utilizing groups is to ADD VALUE. Don't just go in and look for opportunities to sell something or add your program/products. If there is a question you can answer, help out. If someone is looking for a referral you can go to your community rolodex and make a recommendation! Many groups allow you to post things like a Tip Tuesday. Be on the look-out for when you have the opportunity to offer your expertise.

When connecting in groups, don't forget the value of one-on-one connections. When you have the opportunity to connect one-on-one and you feel a true connection, keep it going. Don't forget about those people just because life got busy and you didn't talk for a little while. Circle back and reconnect.

You may also choose to set up your own Facebook group and networking events. If you have a group, you can offer some fun, inspiring, educational, and content-rich posts and events. Have guest speakers in the group to talk about topics that would be of interest and value to your audience.

Currently, I do Spotlight Talks in my group. Inspirational quotes, engaging posts that ask thoughtful questions, Tips of your trade, and polls have had great interaction in my group. Hosting an event within your group for members to network and connect, this can be done occasionally or regularly with coffee chats, speed networking, etc.

Here are some tips to get the most out of online groups:

- Invite people! Some people need the invitation to join an online group or a networking event. So be the one that invites them—either to your own group or another group that you've found valuable.

- Do some research. Who is part of that group? What are the group rules? Opportunities? How did the group start? Investigate the Facebook group and the person you connected with before you meet with them again. Friend them on Facebook after you connect.

- Join 4-6 groups (10 at the most). Any more and you will be overwhelmed trying to keep up with all of them.

- Offer value. Don't just go in and promote yourself. Give referrals. Share helpful information for free. Don't give away your services, but give value every chance you get.

- Make one-on-one connections. If you find someone who you want to connect with, comment on the post that you would love to connect with and will send them a private message.

- If you don't have a calendar link, consider getting one. It makes it so much easier to say "here is a link

to my calendar, pick a time that works for you!"
Rather than going back and forth suggesting times
and trying to find one that works for both parties.

- If you don't have a FB group/community I highly
  recommend starting one. This will create a place for
  your circle to connect and elevate one another.

Connect & Elevate is about bringing people together
to chat, get to know each other through networking and
connecting, coffee chats, masterminds, and ultimately
creating a space for partnerships and collaborations.
When we come together, we all elevate. Adding value
enhances your networking and connecting experience,
nurturing those connections and how to create those
Master Connectors in your business.

Intropreneur in Action

Angela's Story

Angela is one of my very first clients and my friend (Most of the people I connect and network with do eventually become friends.) Angela shares her story about how relationships and networking have changed the way she does business that aligns with her introvert self.

"I am an introvert through and through. Whenever I head into an unfamiliar social situation, I get incredibly anxious and need ample opportunity to recharge afterwards. When I started my business two years ago, I knew networking had to be involved. I assumed the networking process for me would be about as much fun as getting cavities filled at the dentist. Then I met Jen Jones. She truly gets what it's like navigating the networking scene as an introvert. Not only does she understand, but she supports your process in making networking work for you. Jen gives you easy, tangible tips that you can apply right away and always reminds you of your "why" for networking in the first place. Not only does Jen give you tangible tips for while you're networking, but truly takes it to the next level with guidance on what to do after that initial networking interaction. You don't think about the follow-up

until you're in it - then what? Luckily, Jen breaks down in bite-sized chunks how to follow-up with a new connection and authentically cultivate a positive, collaborative relationship with them. Because I've been able to not only network more confidently, but build strong relationships with other female entrepreneurs, the majority of my business comes from word-of-mouth. I love the experience of working with clients that come through this referral method because I know that they're the right clients for me and I'm the right fit for them. It's all thanks to Jen and her passion for helping introverts succeed in networking and connecting with others!"

Angela spends her time rejuvenating after all that connecting, networking, and doing business by taking care of herself.

Here's what she does for your energy, awareness and rejuvenation:

"1) I try to space out things that will deplete my energy between things that don't. For example, I might do an in-person networking event on a Monday, but then work on a design for a client on Tuesday.

2) I try to tap into when I have the most energy during the day and schedule my more challenging tasks around that. For example, doing an in-person site visit takes my time and energy because I'm taking measurements/before photos throughout the home all while talking with the client and drilling down on their design vision. Not to mention traveling to their home has its own level of anxiety. (Will I get lost? Will I get there on time?) Because I know I'm not a morning person, I try to schedule those in the late morning/early afternoon.

3) I give myself the grace to have a day when I do nothing but watch TV and snuggle with my dog if I need that day."

-4-

Getting Comfortable with Shining Your Light

Chapter 12

Referral Relationship Strategy

In 2004, I started my real estate business. I sold my own house and thought this was easy! I got into the real estate business so I could have a flexible schedule, make a decent living with endless opportunities, and spend time with my kids and not have to work "for the man." What I didn't realize is real estate was a perfect job for that outgoing, charismatic friend, not me! Or so I thought. It took me a few years to figure out that I wasn't like most of the agents in my office. I hated door knocking and cold calling, which I did very little of in the beginning and none of that in the last decade.

It became evident that my skills and introverted self liked to work with the people I already knew and their referrals. From that moment on, I decided if I was going to "make it" in real estate, I needed to shift my attention to the people I already knew and build my business on repeat clients and referrals. Knowing what you want to do and then implementing it can be difficult. To make implementation easier, I developed the Referral Relationship Strategy.

The Referral Relationship Strategy includes taking your introvert gifts and combining them with your business mission and vision. It gives you the outline to run your business your way. Shining in the entrepreneurial world doesn't take hustle, where you burn out by pushing hard and making deep sacrifices of self and family. Rather than requiring this depletion of energy, this strategy feels good and gets you the results you're looking for in less time and energy.

The Referral Relationship Strategy includes Four Steps:

1. Identify & Connect

2. Love & Appreciation

3. Ask & Refer

4. Shine & Give Back

As you go through each step, write your implementation strategy.

1. Identify & Connect

Identifying and Connecting with your top 25 Master Connectors (or more, if you decide there are more) and then organize the remaining in the second and third circles of the bullseye. The goal is to always be connecting, you decide if you want to do a group or 1:1, set up a coffee chat or block out time to meet 1:1 with your Master Connectors.

Create the opportunity to meet new people. Add them to your circle if they are the right fit. These opportunities present themselves in many ways. Being aware of what brings you the most joy is key to networking and connecting. What lights you up? 1:1 meetings? Attending a small networking event? Attending a large networking event? Asking for a referral from your circle about where they meet people? Do you have a hobby that you can get involved with to meet new people? Gym? Art, like paint or pottery? Are there groups (in-person or online) of people that you may have things in common with? You can absolutely look for things and activities to find the people you want to add to your circle.

Connect with those in your circle that you have not talked to in awhile. Make a list of 10 people to reconnect with to nurture the relationship. You get busy and may fall off the connection wagon or maybe you took a break to be a hermit for a bit.

2. Love & Appreciation

It's all about love, appreciation, and value! I could talk about love and appreciation for many pages! (Oh wait! I did in chapter 8!) When sharing love and appreciation, it is important to know what lights you up and brings you joy when you are talking about giving value to others. If you just gave what you thought people wanted, especially as an introvert, you would end up drained, burnt out and ready for multiple vacations!

There are two categories to work with. One is business promotion and the other is personal development/advancement. As you think about the things you can do to love up on your community, find the ones that bring you the most joy. If it brings you joy, you better bet the receiver will feel your joy, excitement, appreciation and know your intentions are pure, good, and valuable. Let's look at each of these categories.

1. Business promotion that has value – for example a masterclass with your top 5 tips.

2. Personal Development/Advancement – for example a journal (although this may be part of business promotion too depending on your business).

When we think of these two categories, we want to offer value that people appreciate and want to reciprocate. If we are always giving top tips and promoting our business every single time, it doesn't feel authentic nor joyful. Always selling is not the way of an introvert, or at least an Intropreneur. Be mindful as you set up what "value" you give to your circle. Ask yourself, is this of value to my circle? Don't get me wrong, there may be things that some of your circle may not see as valuable, it just doesn't connect for them, that's ok. Keep trying and the more you give the more people will see you love, appreciate and care about them.

Follow-up can be hard for so many people, not just introverts. Knowing that your follow-up is done with good intentions and you clearly communicated to the other person that you would be following up. Staying in touch is an asset and an introvert gift we have because we value deep relationships. What better way to create the community with people you want than to follow up? Being consistent with this follow-up will help you to create a habit of staying top of mind with your community. See chapter 10 to go more in depth with follow-up.

3. Ask & Refer

Asking for referrals can be difficult at times or most times, depending on who you are and your comfort level. When you are offering so much value to your people, it comes natural in conversations to ask for referrals. There are plenty of opportunities to ask for referrals and give them. This is the reason for giving to your top 25 Master Connectors. It is important for your confidence to bring forth these amazing people that you are most comfortable with talking to and people who won't be judging you for how you ask for referrals, especially if you are a new business owner. Finding your joy in asking for referrals. This may look different for many. The spoken word is most desirable for me, as I can gauge their body language, the subject and tone of the conversation.

I'd also encourage people to ask each other for referrals, post in your community, or encourage them to reach out to you when they have a need.

We also want to be asking for testimonials. Your clients and customers want to rave about their experience. Give them the opportunity to do so and make it easy. For example, if you are looking for a Google or Facebook review, give them the links and let them know they can copy and paste. If someone left a review on one and not the other, message them and just ask them to copy, paste and post to the platform they didn't review on. These are just a couple examples of asks.

One of the biggest gifts you can give to someone else is a referral to their product or service. In almost every conversation, I am on the lookout for who of my people I can refer. You should always be ready to refer someone from your business circle when the opportunity arises. This not only brings forth them and their business, it is an opportunity to elevate them. You can also be proactive with this by showcasing or featuring one of your business owner/entrepreneurs that are in your circle. This could be done by email, in your facebook group, if you have one, print mail, an event you are hosting, online series or podcast you host, informal or formal partnership or collaboration, the list goes on.

Rewarding referrals with a handwritten note and a small gift. This gift could be a gift certificate, a book, a journal, anything that shows that you know these people well. They are like your BFFs who use the information you have gathered on your Master Connectors to give them what they like! For example, if one of your master connectors loves to grab their latte at their favorite coffee shop, then get them a gift card from that place.

What if they love unique jewelry pieces? You must know someone in your business connections that provides gift certificates for their unique jewelry pieces? You bet you do! And if you don't, then get networking and asking for a referral for just that. Remember that you are not only providing products and services to your clients and potential clients, but you are also a resource for your people. You are the one that people will come to when they are looking for a referral.

Teach them how to help you. First, remember to ask for their business and their referrals. Be specific when you are asking. Make it personal, don't cut and paste or script it. Make sure it sounds like you. Something like, I appreciate your support in my business, who do you know that I can help?

Think about ways to elevate your circle through connections like referrals, partners, collaborations, events, sponsors. This isn't about selling your or some other person's service or product, it's about connecting them because you are offering them what they have asked for. Your partners are willing to share your work, program, service, product with their own circle via social media, email, making a personal connection etc. Always be ready to ask for and give referrals.

4. Shine & Give Back

Shine, the spotlight is all on you! Some introverts are ok with the spotlight depending on the audience. Other introverts will avoid it like the plague. This is more reason to implement the Referral Relationship Strategy (RRS). It gives you the comfort of your circle.

The "how" to get new people in your circle is also part of your selection from the RRS. There are benefits to going to networking events and meetings to meet new people. I've also seen where 1:1s have worked well for others, and of course then there's the model of doing both but limiting the events/meetings with larger crowds. You choose how you want to be visible to the world.

What I'd encourage you to do is look at your vision and what you want to bring into this world. Stepping into the spotlight and being visible has its impact on this world.

You become visible to your circle, you are the one that leads these people, your visibility within your circle sets you up to be out in the world.

Showing up and being seen also gives you the opportunity to elevate your business by giving back. You are not only giving back to your circle, but you are in a position to give back on a larger scale. What's your deep passion to give back? This could relate to your current business or it could be something that you have always wanted to do and now that you are in a position of influence and have the income, you now can have the impact in the world. How will you give back?

This could start small and grow as you and your business grow. Supporting a cause will also bring your circle together and it can bring people from your immediate community, whether geographical or online.

Create a strategy that you can implement and have accountability. There are times when I can be accountable to myself. Many times when I am implementing something new or changing the way I am doing things, I really want some accountability. There's something to be said for when people come together to cheer each other on but also keep them accountable to what goals they set for themselves.

The Referral Relationship Strategy follows the same principles as what we've been talking about throughout this book. The heart of this strategy starts with your authentic self, the joy you have for your life and business, and the relationships in your circle. Increasing your referral business will increase your income. It comes down to your bottom line.

We are in business to live our best life, for me that means vacations, time off, and being available to my family and friends. How best to spend money is on the people we already know, your circle. By investing in your circle of people, you are having a bigger impact than trying to get the attention of people who do not know you. Your expenses will go down and your income will go up. Your circle of people are more likely to refer your business.

Instead of looking for the next shiny way to get in front of new people that might be interested in what you have to offer, how about spending that time with the people you already know and loving on them. In the end your income will increase from building a referral business.

Relationship Referral Strategy Action Items

- List 25 (or more) of your Master Connectors.
- List out all your second and third Connectors.
- Add one new person to your circle weekly/monthly.
- Attend one networking event/meeting weekly/monthly.
- Schedule 1:1 meetings weekly.
- Schedule 1 biz connection weekly.
- Brainstorm five to ten ways you can love on your circle.

- Choose five people you can love on every week.
- Set up a Customer Relationship Management (CRM system).
- Schedule 1:1 with a Master Connector weekly/monthly.
- Consider planning a gathering for your circle.
- Investigate one new opportunity (Podcast, guest speaker, speaking, give a talk in a Facebook Group).
- Pick your top five Master Connectors and ask for referrals
- Ask for testimonials.
- Ask your current clients for referrals.

Chapter 13

Collaborations

Now let's talk about collaborations. This is a great opportunity to bring amazing like-minded, successful people together. They come along with you, if you are spearheading or you are part of a collaboration led by someone else. When we come together the elevation is so much more powerful than going it alone!

Whenever you have the opportunity to work with another business owner, it elevates everyone involved. Take the opportunity to ask or invite.

If you are asked to collaborate with other business owners, consider doing it. If you feel they are a good fit for you and you for them, give it some thought. Even if it is out of your comfort zone.

There are endless ways to collaborate. I will share my favorites, those of my clients and group members:

Joint Marketing - There are a couple ways you can approach joint marketing. 1) You and another business owner that have complimentary businesses that make sense showcase one another with the other's audience via mail, email, social media, and other media. 2) You and multiple businesses helping each other by joint marketing to one another's businesses. In this case, they could be complimentary or it could be an effort to market small businesses, etc.

Joint Giveaways/Contests - Similar to Joint Marketing, this just adds a layer of a giveaway/contest to win something as part of the offerings. This is a way to get new people to become part of your circle, nurture the people in your circle and the other businesses circle(s), it gives the opportunity to win something and we all love to win free stuff, or most of us!

Networking Events - Whether your businesses compliment each other or not, hosting a collaborative networking event with one or more businesses can help you bring your circles together to meet each other. These events definitely can feel magical. People who were meant to meet each other are connected. It's a time where you can see the connections happening. There are cases where there are mismatches but that is the risk you take when participating in any event, in-person or online. Some examples of types of networking events that can be created are: speed networking, masterminds, and general networking with a speaker/topic.

Summits/Online Series - These events are typically with several other people, mostly business owners wanting to give value to the audience. Bringing people together to share their gifts and passion with the world in a format that is educational, reflective, and connective. Giving the audience a free gift from each speaker, allows them to choose what they want to tap into, what speaker pulled them closer and spoke to their heart.

Podcasts/Live Shows - Podcasts are a simple and easy way to tell your story and allow others to do the same. If you have a show you invite guests to speak and share their work. This gets their (and your) message out into an audience of many. Follow your heart when inviting guests on your show and it will bring value, love, and light into the world. If you have ever been invited or solicited to be a guest, find those hosts that align with your message and passion.

Partnerships in Programs and Events - This is a collaboration where you are either asked or you volunteer your time to help promote someone else's program, event, etc. In this case, it is usually another business owner that trusts you, you are both aligned in your values, mission, vision and they are looking for your help to spread their message about what they are doing in their business. The person asking usually provides you with all the marketing copy, graphics, etc. All you need to do is take action - facebook post, email to your circle, etc. There have been times when I've raised my hand and said, "If you need help spreading the word, let me know."

Referral Partners - This could range from very formal contract-based partners to an informal partnership that refer each other. There are a wide variety of ways to set up a referral partnership. Give yourself some time to think about what is a win-win moving forward.

Sponsorships - An opportunity to financially support a cause, event, groups, sports, etc. usually in exchange for marketing of your business. The marketing ranges from the ability to share your business live with guests of the event to your logo on a sign. There are so many ways to give back to the sponsors, so if you are the one putting together the benefits of a sponsorship, put yourself in the sponsors shoes and think about how you can offer the biggest return on their investment. Most people and businesses sponsor to support the "cause" and it feels good to offer value to them when they do!

There are many reasons why we collaborate with other people, whether it's one person or a group. One business has an impact, once you add in more business owners the impact doesn't just double it really has a massive impact.

What collaboration will you lead or be part of?

Chapter 14

Getting Started

The four pillars outlined in this book provide guidance as to the wholeness of growing and nurturing your relationships and your business to have the lifestyle you want, both in your income and enjoyment. If you are feeling a bit overwhelmed and not sure where to start, the simplest advice I will give you is start on chapter one and work your way through.

If you feel like you already have some of this nailed, then pick one thing to work on next. You decide the time frame. I usually say 30 days but this is about what lifestyle you want to create, so you get to decide.

The results you will see will include more authentic relationships with yourself and other people (family, friends, clients, circle), you'll be an expert in no time when it comes to your energy awareness and management, and you'll see your lifestyle align when your business has more referrals, repeat business, and people who want to be in your energy.

We all want fulfilling lives with lifestyles we decide are right for us and our families. I help clients 1) Know themselves better and align with your natural strengths as an introvert, values, goals, mission and vision so that you can leverage your energy and experience deeper, more joy-filled connections. 2) Bring energetic awareness to your life and business to be able to do it all, without actually doing it all: the uncompromised introvert. 3) And connect with your network on a deeper level and cultivate ongoing, authentic relationships that yield consistent referrals and repeat business.

This is all evident in the client stories I've shared in this book. My own success story has inspired many women Intropreneurs and the reason this book was born. Putting this work into the world is giving more people steps to take to move through their life more fulfilled, energized and nurturing meaningful, deep relationships, both personal and professional.

Here's to defining your success, using your introvert gifts, awareness of your energy and having a business that fits you and your authentic self. Wishing you much success and the gratitude I have for you picking up this book, reading it, and now ready to take the next step in your life and business. With a loving heart, clear mind, and ready to shine more light into the world, I wish you the lifestyle you desire!

Acknowledgements

I'd like to express my deepest thanks to my clients and community who have shown me over the years how important deep, meaningful relationships really are in fulfilling my life and business. They have shown me over and over again how profound referrals and repeat business is in my business and theirs. Thank you to all the introverted entrepreneurs who started asking me questions about networking back in 2019 that stimulated the need for Intropreneur. We didn't know then that it would become a book!

To my rock and husband Rob who has been there every step of the way making sure I had the support I needed to be successful not only in my business but in our lives too. This journey we are on puts a smile on my face. I'm so fortunate to have him by my side as one of my biggest supporters and cheerleaders.

To my daughter Haley who even helped search for possible book cover ideas. She continues to cheer me on and wants a signed copy to put in a "frame." To my son Hunter who made me realize I was putting limits on myself. And to my youngest son Kellen, who would snuggle up on me as I had my laptop on my lap writing and editing the book. It was just what I needed.

To Liz, my publisher/editor who is patient, kind, and reminded me that "she's got me." Liz helped me get my head around the whole process. This book is a gift to the world that wouldn't be possible without her expertise and guidance.

To Dr. Davia Shepherd for inviting me into her circle and coaching me on visibility, giving me opportunities to speak, share my message, and put me in the spotlight so I could share and shine.

About Jen Jones

Jen Jones has been an entrepreneur for over 20 years, both as an owner of a boutique real estate agency and as a business coach consultant. She has successfully scaled businesses by building deep, meaningful relationships with her clients that inspire repeat business and referrals. She lives by the motto 'go deep not wide.'

Jen guides her clients through the four-step process to harness their introvert self, have more energy awareness so they can align their business and life with meaningful connections, elevate relationships, which produce more referral and repeat business with the right people.

As the mom of three kids, she gets how important it is to balance having a family and a fulfilling business that doesn't drain your battery or burn you out. When she's not showing houses, helping clients or volunteering, you'll find her with her family and friends. She enjoys her alone time doing yoga, honing her intuition skills, meditating, and journaling.

ConnectandElevate.com

Praise for Jen Jones

"I am so happy to have found the space that Master
Connector Jen Jones has created for introverted female
entrepreneurs in Connect & Elevate. Since she is also one
of us, she knows what we go through to do some of the
all-important connecting/networking activities that are
critical to our success. She breaks it down into easy steps
that we all can do and helps build our confidence to put
ourselves out there. She helps us see how our strengths can
be used to network comfortably, and make the sales we
need for our businesses to grow. I highly recommend her
for ALL introverted businesswomen who know they need
to connect in order to elevate."
April Goff Brown

"Thank you, Jen, for creating and holding space that
empowers women to reflect and step more fully
into their authentic selves."
Susan Swain

Jen Jones

Connect with Jen

Connect & Elevate
https://www.facebook.com/groups/391015638165931

https://www.linkedin.com/in/jen-jones-58994212/

About Green Heart Living

Green Heart Living's mission is to make the world a more loving and peaceful place, one person at a time. Green Heart Living Press publishes inspirational books and stories of transformation, making the world a more loving and peaceful place, one book at a time.

Whether you have an idea for an inspirational book and want support through the writing process – or your book is already written and you are looking for a publishing path – Green Heart Living can help you get your book out into the world.

You can meet Green Heart authors on the Green Heart Living YouTube channel and the Green Heart Living Podcast.

www.greenheartliving.com

Green Heart Living Publications

Be the Beacon

Success in Any Season

Embrace Your Space

Your Daily Dose of PositiviDee

Redefining Masculinity

*Growing Smarter: Collaboration Secrets
to Transform Your Income and Impact*

Transformation 2020

Transformation 2020 Companion Journal

The Great Pause: Blessings & Wisdom from COVID-19

The Great Pause Journal

Love Notes: Daily Wisdom for the Soul

*Green Your Heart, Green Your World: Avoid Burnout,
Save the World and Love Your Life*

Made in USA - North Chelmsford, MA
1305324_9781954493193
02.17.2022 1717